THE FALL
OF HITLER'S
FORTRESS CITY

'The city fell in ruins and burned. The German positions were smashed, the trenches ploughed up, embrasures were levelled with the ground, companies were buried, the signal systems torn apart and the ammunition stores destroyed. Clouds of smoke lay over the remnants of the houses of the inner city. On the streets were strewn fragments of masonry, shot-up vehicles and the bodies of horses and human beings.'

Michael Wieck,
A Childhood under Hitler and Stalin

THE FALL
OF HITLER'S
FORTRESS CITY

The Battle for Königsberg,
1945

ISABEL DENNY

CASEMATE
Philadelphia & Newbury
A Greenhill Book

Published in the United States of America in 2009 by
CASEMATE
908 Darby Road, Havertown, PA 19083

and in the United Kingdom by
CASEMATE
17 Cheap Street, Newbury, RG14 5DD

🌳 *A Greenhill Book*

ISBN 978-1-935149-20-0

LLYFRGELLOEDD SIR DDINBYCH	
C46 0000 0462 534	
HJ	25-Nov-2010
940.542172	£14.99
RL	

Cataloging in publication data is available from the
Library of Congress and the British Library.

First published in 2007 by Greenhill Books, London.

For a complete list of Casemate titles, please contact:

United States of America
Casemate Publishers
Telephone (610) 853-9131, Fax (610) 853-9146
E-mail casemate@casematepublishing.com
Website www.casematepublishing.com

United Kingdom
Casemate-UK
Telephone (01635) 231091, Fax (01635) 41619
E-mail casemate-uk@casematepublishing.co.uk
Website www.casematepublishing.co.uk

PRINTED AND BOUND IN THE UNITED STATES OF AMERICA

CONTENTS

ILLUSTRATIONS

MAPS

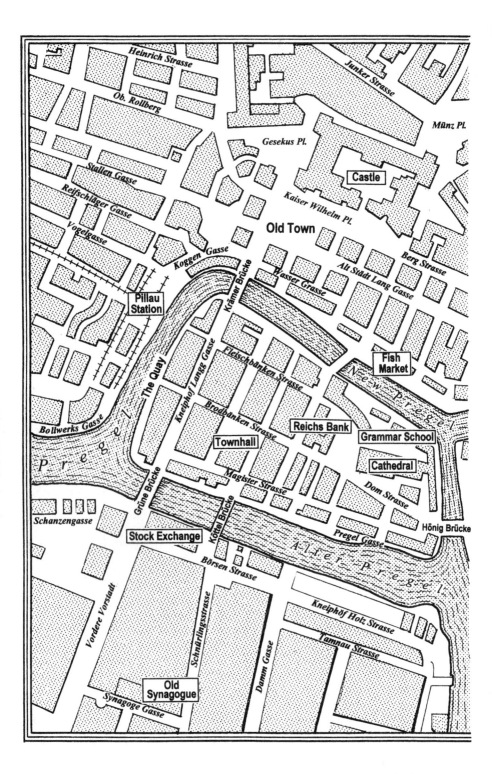

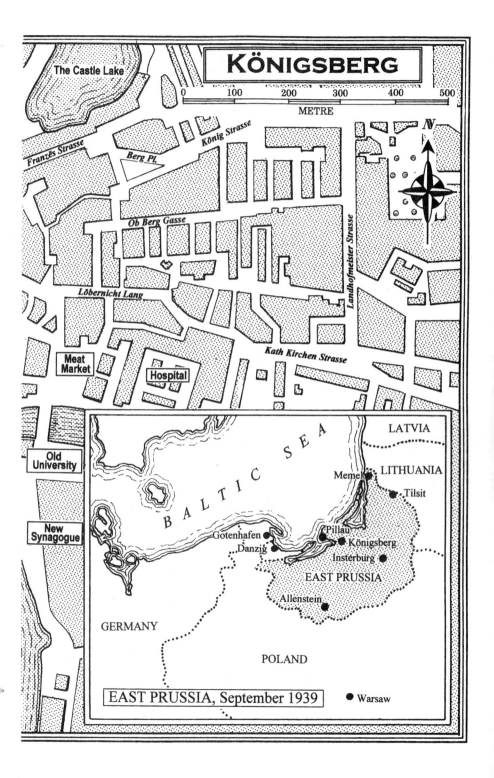

A KÖNIGSBERG CHRONOLOGY

The Early Years

1255 The Teutonic Knights begin to build a castle on the banks of the River Pregel.

1257 The castle site is given the name Königsberg.

1286 The 'Old Town' is founded around the castle walls.

1327 The Kneiphof Island in the River Pregel is settled.

1333 Foundation stone of the new cathedral is laid.

1457–1525 Königsberg Castle becomes the chief residence of the Grand Duke of the Teutonic Knights.

1525 Königsberg becomes the capital of the Duchy of Brandenburg after Albert of Brandenburg dissolves the Teutonic Order and transfers its territory to the secular Duchy of Prussia.

1540 Arrival of first Jewish settlers.

1544 Foundation of the Albertina University in Königsberg.

1618 Unification of Prussia and Brandenburg.

1660 Berlin becomes the capital city of Prussia and Brandenburg.

The Prussian Kingdom

1701 Elector Frederick III of Brandenburg is crowned King Frederick I of Prussia in Königsberg.

1709–11 Plague kills a quarter of the population of Königsberg.

1712 First Jewish students admitted to the University.

1724 Birth of Immanuel Kant.

1756 Synagogue opens in Königsberg.

1853 The railway comes to Königsberg.

1861 William I of Prussia crowned in Königsberg Cathedral.

The German Empire

1878 Königsberg becomes the official capital of East Prussia.

1893 Opening of large new synagogue in the city.

1895 First electric tramway in Germany opens in the city.

1914–18 First World War.

Weimar Interlude

1919 Versailles Peace Treaty cuts East Prussia off from the rest of Germany.

1920 Opening of *Ostmesse* trade fair site in Königsberg.

1922 Construction of airport.

1928 Erich Koch becomes Nazi Party Gauleiter of East Prussia.

Into the Abyss

1933 Hitler becomes German Chancellor and pays official visit to Königsberg.

1936 Re-occupation of the Rhineland.

1938 Anschluss with Austria; Hitler visits Königsberg again; *Kristallnacht.*

1939 Occupation of Memel; dismemberment of Czechoslovakia and Poland and outbreak of Second World War.

June 1941 Operation Barbarossa – the German invasion of the Soviet Union – begins.

August 1942 Assault on Stalingrad begins.

February 1943 German Army surrenders at Stalingrad.

March 1943 First Allied discussion on the future of East Prussia.

November 1943 Teheran conference; Allies agree that East Prussia and Memel will be permanently confiscated from Germany at the end of the war.

June 1944 Beginning of Operation Bagration – the Soviet destruction of the German Army Group Centre.

July 1944 Failure of the Stauffenberg plot to assassinate Hitler.

August 1944 British air raids on Königsberg destroy large parts of the city.

October 1944 Allies agree that Königsberg region will be ceded to USSR after the war; Red Army attacks Memel; formation of Volkssturm – a Home Guard to help in the defence of Germany; first Russian attacks on East Prussia.

1945

January Launch of main Soviet attack on East Prussia; East Prussia cut off from the rest of the Reich; Erich Koch flees from Königsberg.

29 January Beginning of first siege of Königsberg.

30 January Sinking of the *Wilhelm Gustloff* with the loss of nearly 9,000 lives; Hitler broadcasts to the German people for the last time.

20 February First siege of Königsberg broken.

6 April Beginning of second and final siege of Königsberg; destruction of most of the city.

9 April Königsberg surrenders to Soviet Army.

16 April Surrender of East Prussia.

30 April Death of Adolf Hitler.

8 May Germany surrenders.

Aftermath

July 1945 Potsdam conference confirms Soviet annexation of Königsberg.

July 1946 Königsberg renamed Kaliningrad.

1947–8 Remaining Germans evacuated from Kaliningrad.

1946 Kaliningrad is incorporated into the Soviet Union.

1969 Remains of Königsberg Castle destroyed to make way for the House of Soviets.

1991 Kaliningrad reopened to visitors from abroad; Lithuania becomes independent, cutting Kaliningrad off from the rest of Russia.

2005 The 750th anniversary of the foundation of Königsberg is celebrated by many of its former inhabitants.

PREFACE

I met a traveller from an antique land
Who said: Two vast and trunkless legs of stone
Stand in the desert. Near them, on the sand,
Half sunk, a shattered visage lies, whose frown
And wrinkled lip, and sneer of cold command,
Tell that its sculptor well those passions read,
Which yet survive, stamped on these lifeless things,
The hand that mocked them, and the heart that fed:
And on the pedestal these words appear:
'My name is Ozymandias, King of Kings:
Look upon my works, ye Mighty, and despair!'
Nothing beside remains. Round the decay
Of that colossal wreck, boundless and bare
The lone and level sands stretch far away.

P. B. Shelley

There are many books about the military campaigns on the Eastern Front at the end of the Second World War. There is, however, little available in English on the effects on the lives of the people who lived through the Soviet invasion of Germany's most easterly province, East Prussia, and its capital city, Königsberg; few are aware of its fate after the war ended.

The historic Hanseatic city of Königsberg was almost completely destroyed by British bombs and Russian assault between August 1944 and April 1945 and what little remained was demolished in the months after it was taken over by the Soviet Union in 1945. In the 1970s I visited Poland and from the top of the cathedral of Frombork (the former Frauenburg) on the Baltic coast, it was just possible to see along the curve in the coast to a few lone buildings where once this beautiful and prosperous city had dominated the Baltic coastline. At the time I knew little about what had brought about its terrible end, but some years later, in western Germany, I met many people who had been forced to leave after the Russians invaded and I was moved by their memories of their beautiful pre-war city and what happened to it when the Russians came. Most were elderly women who had been children when they had to flee and the descriptions of what had occurred forced me to confront the fact that, although Germany had been responsible for the Second World War, the experiences of these civilians were so horrifying that they demanded investigation.

In 1939 the German province of East Prussia was a quiet rural region on the eastern side of the Baltic Sea. It had been isolated from the rest of the country when the Polish Corridor was created by the Versailles peacemakers. Its economy suffered severely as a result, but it still remained a peaceful and pleasant place to live and this land 'of endless woods and a thousand lakes' remained largely unaffected by the outbreak of the Second World War. Life in the countryside and in the provincial capital, Königsberg, continued much as usual.

The eventual fate of East Prussia and Königsberg lay in Adolf Hitler's hands. From the day he began his attack on the Soviet Union in 1941, in a war which was intended to exterminate or enslave the people he called the 'degenerate' Slavs, the destruction of the fortress city Königsberg and the loss of East Prussia became almost inevitable. In June 1944 the Soviets launched a huge counter-offensive against

Germany on the Eastern Front, intending to drive Hitler's armies out of Poland, the Baltic provinces, and Belorussia – and then to march through Germany to Berlin. By the late summer the Soviets had already reached the East Prussian border and were making reconnaissance flights over Königsberg. The destruction of the city began, however, with two enormous bombing raids by the British RAF that August during which half of the old town was destroyed. Thousands were killed and tens of thousands were made homeless.

The Russians made their first inroads into Prussia in October 1944, and it soon became clear that the Red Army was intent on exacting revenge on the German people for the millions of Russian deaths in the war. As the Red Army advanced, the terrified inhabitants fled from these eastern borderlands, despite orders to stay and defend the Fatherland, making for the coast or Königsberg. In November there was a respite as Russian forces regrouped but the attack was renewed in January 1945 and this time the advance swept through the whole province as the desperate population tried to escape in one of the coldest winters of the mid-twentieth century. Königsberg eventually surrendered on 9 April and what was left of the city was razed. Its buildings were eventually replaced by unattractive and utilitarian Stalinist blocks which still tarnish the landscape.

An old Baltic legend describes a lost coastal city called Winetha which was supposedly destroyed for the sins and errors of its inhabitants who had grown hard and proud. On fine and calm days mariners claimed to see the city under the waters of the Baltic, with its silver ramparts and marble columns. Every Good Friday Winetha rose briefly from the sea with its towers, palaces and walls in place and than sank into oblivion again.

Visitors to Kaliningrad frequently experience a strange feeling that, under the ugly town which exists today, the old city of Königsberg is lying in wait, ready to resurface when the time is right. In 2006 Moscow declared it wanted to turn the region into 'the Russian Hong Kong', and designated Kaliningrad a Special Economic Zone. The old Hanseatic city can probably never be reconstructed in its full glory and we can only try to conjure up a picture of what it must have been like to live in this fine and historic Baltic port in the years before Hitler wrought havoc on the German nation.

As with Königsberg/Kaliningrad itself, many of the places mentioned in this book have had more than one name. The text that follows normally uses the German name for places in and around the former East Prussia. Modern names for these places are given in the *Appendix* on p. 249.

Passages from Michael Wieck's *A Childhood Under Hitler and Stalin* (English-language edition of *Zeugnis vom Untergang Königsbergs*) are reprinted by permission of The University of Wisconsin Press and Universitätsverlag Winter, Heidelberg.

My thanks are due to the many émigrés from the eastern part of Germany who have shared their thoughts and recollections with me, to Herr Lorenz Grimoni of the Königsberg archives in Duisburg, and to my husband for his patience in helping me through the intricacies of the German language when my own understanding failed.

Isabel Denny

INTRODUCTION

January 1945 was one of the coldest in living memory in north-east Europe. Each night the temperature fell to –25 degrees Celsius and by day it rarely rose above freezing. The ground froze and the Baltic Sea was covered with a solid layer of ice. On 24 January the advancing Soviet Army severed all road and railway routes to the west and the province of East Prussia was cut off from the rest of the German Reich.

In this arctic weather hundreds of thousands of civilians packed their possessions onto sledges and horse-drawn carts and fled from the Russians. The German Army was in retreat and the Red Army advanced so rapidly towards the coast that there were only two routes of escape. One was from the Baltic port of Pillau just a few kilometres from Königsberg, where a fleet of vessels waited to transport those who managed to get there to the safety of the west. The other was over a frozen lagoon, the Frisches Haff, beyond which was a narrow sandy spit called the Frisches Nehrung. The Nehrung would lead the refugees to Gotenhafen or Danzig – and to another escape route by sea.

The main route onto the Haff was at Heiligenbeil, which bordered the narrowest stretch of the lagoon. The roads approaching the little town were packed with queues of terrified refugees. Their rickety carts and sledges were loaded with their household possessions and the town was crowded with civilians and soldiers. Each morning, as daylight broke, columns of carts, wagons, animals and people stepped apprehensively onto the ice of the Haff. Progress was painfully slow across the ten kilometres which led to the Nehrung.

The German Army had marked out a route with wooden stakes to show where the ice was safe, and thousands of refugees trudged across this pathway. An eyewitness later recalled the silence of the trekkers as an indescribable ghostly procession with eyes full of misery and wretchedness and quiet resignation. The slow-moving line showed up clearly on the ice and the women, children and elderly people who made up the majority of the refugees were a sitting target for the low-flying Russian aircraft which crossed and re-crossed the frozen waste. The route was littered with abandoned luggage, upturned carts and the corpses of those who had not finished the journey. Children, the elderly and the sick lay helplessly in open wagons in soaked and freezing straw or under wet dirty blankets. They were the main victims of exposure to the icy weather but many others fell through the ice or were mortally wounded by Russian artillery fire, their blood discolouring the frozen surface of the lake. Their corpses lay all around in grotesque positions. For most refugees, the distant fir-tree-lined Nehrung took two or three days to reach and as the horses grew tired people began to throw goods from their wagons to make them lighter.

Those who made it to the Nehrung faced a long trudge along a narrow sandy road, which had originally been built to take small fishing wagons, but now had to cope with the endless civilian wagon trains and with military lorries carrying wounded servicemen. At this time of the year the track was covered with deep snow which the wind blew into massive drifts. None of the small fishing villages along the Nehrung had the resources to deal with such huge numbers of people.

They overflowed with starving refugees; there was no bread, no food for the animals and there was no fresh water. Few travellers wanted to talk to each other about the events that had led them to pack up at short notice and abandon their homes and villages as the Soviet armies approached. None of them want to think about the fate of those who failed to get away or had been overtaken by the Russians and had been robbed, raped, captured and in some instances killed.

When the refugees reached Gotenhafen or one of the other ports, they joined thousands waiting on the dockside, under repeated Russian attack, desperately trying to get away. Crowding towards the gangplanks, they pushed their way onto vessels which quickly became dangerously overloaded. Many had to leave behind what remained of their meagre possessions. The sea was frozen and ships leaving the harbour had to steer clear of huge ice floes as well as try to avoid attacks from the air or from submarines. Those who managed to get away were aware that they faced a most uncertain future in war-damaged western Germany.

In the first four months of 1945, 2.5 million East Prussians tried to escape by these routes and it is probable that a million of them died, in the cold, on the ice, in the sea or at the hands of the Russians. Shocking though these numbers are, they were insignificant when compared with the 11.5 million civilians and 10.7 million soldiers lost by the Russians in their four-year war against the Third Reich.

Chapter One

A LAND OF
QUIET AUSTERITY

In 1945 the German province of East Prussia and its capital city, Königsberg, ceased to exist. Before the Second World War East Prussia had reached far into Eastern Europe and was known to its inhabitants as 'the land of dark forests and crystal lakes'.[1]

The Masurian Lakes, in the east of the region, were a haven for wildlife and the lakes were so numerous that local people referred to them as *Auglein* – 'little eyes' – sparkling amongst the dense woods. The natural instinct of the people was to regard East Prussia as the most beautiful place in all of Germany, but it was not spectacular countryside and its charm really lay in its isolation, its backwardness and its atmosphere of undisturbed solitude.

Most of its inhabitants lived, as they had done for hundreds of years, in small self-sufficient communities in and around the great estates of the Prussian land-owning classes, the *Junker*. Their lives revolved around the farming year and the changing season; their meagre incomes came from cereal farming, dairy herds and timber. There was little opulence, but there was an atmosphere of modest prosperity, which resulted from hard and patient work. 'The land,' wrote an English visitor in 1938, 'emanated an atmosphere of quiet austerity, as though the people were perpetually hardened to meet the adversities of nature and the challenge of the nearby frontiers.'[2] Even in the 1920s the difference between the town and country dwellers of East Prussia was pronounced and it was rare for estate owners to own a town property. Only the main highways which led directly to the towns were made up; most roads were dusty cart tracks lined with chestnut, beech and silver birch trees, and travelling by road was slow, reflecting the unhurried character of a province which was still essentially rural.

Life in the countryside followed what Marion Gräfin von Dönhoff has called 'the rhythm of the seasons'.[3] The East Prussian winters were long and hard but also the most peaceful season for hard-working labourers. Nevertheless, despite the beauty of the snowy landscape, spring was always eagerly awaited. The end of winter was marked by the snow slipping from the trees: 'At first' wrote the East Prussian novelist, Ernst Wiechert, 'like a veil of dust and later in long white streamers, which were blown through the forests,'[4] and then spring came like an 'explosion', as Max Fürst puts it, with the air 'fizzing like champagne'.[5] The storks, lapwings and starlings returned from their winter migration, heralding the stifling days of hot summers when the corn and rye ripened in fields surrounded by dark forests. In the autumn, after the harvest had been gathered in and the leaves had reddened, came a season of heavy rain and a still and silent countryside, which seemed unchanging and unchanged.

The coastline of East Prussia was picturesque. It curved north-east from the mouth of the River Vistula, around the Gulf of Danzig to the city of Memel (now Klaipeda in Lithuania). It was a region of pine-fringed, sandy beaches and wide river mouths. Much of this section of the Baltic coast is protected by two long sandbanks which each enclose large shallow lagoons of brackish water, which are home to thousands of birds in summer.

The western sandbank, the Frisches Nehrung, extends north from Danzig to the mouth of the Pregel estuary, a distance of nearly a hundred kilometres. Despite it being only 200 metres wide for much of its length, tiny fishing villages were scattered along the sandbar. It encloses a land-locked lagoon, the Frisches Haff, which is up to a dozen kilometres wide. Frauenburg Cathedral, where Copernicus (who called his native city the 'remotest place on earth') is buried, dominated the inland shore of the Haff. From the towers of this imposing brick church there was a magnificent view along the coast to Königsberg. Between the Frisches Nehrung and the northern sandbar is the region known before the war as Samland. It is also known as the Amber Coast because the tide frequently deposits great lumps of the fossilised resin, a prized mineral, along its shores and amber remains one of the main exports of the region.

The north-eastern sandbar, the Kurisches Nehrung (or Curonian Spit), was even more impressive. It is an isolated 100-kilometre thread of sand extending from the Samland Peninsula to the mouth of the River Memel. Its air is full of the mingled scents of sea and pine and the nearby forests are home to wild boar, elk and deer. Before the First World War a few of the sparse population still spoke Kurish, a dialect related to the Lettish language. In the 1920s and 1930s the Spit was a favourite holiday destination of the people of the region who liked to visit it every year. The slogan of the East German Railway Union was 'To the Seagulls and the Sea' and it ran frequent trains to the most popular resort, Cranz. The rickety 14.03 from Königsberg North Station to Cranz was a popular choice which ran directly to the sea in just over half an hour. It rattled through the Fritzener forest and the flat agricultural land of the Samland Peninsula with its windows wide open, making its way to what was popularly regarded as the best bathing resort on the Baltic coast. Nidden was another much-loved holiday spot and one of the most attractive villages in the Baltic coast.

Tied up in these harbours were clumsy broad wooden fishing boats, which were designed to cope with the shallow waters of the Kurisches Haff. Photographs from the 1920s show fishermen ankle-deep in water landing the plentiful fish and women drying the catch on nets stretched out on the tideless shore.[6] Beyond the village the peaceful beaches were surrounded by stretches of shifting dunes of fine golden sand, which gave the impression of the great sandy waves of the desert. The shifting dunes were loosely packed mountains of sand blown by the wind which on stormy days could reach up to eighty metres in height. Behind the bare dunes were tranquil grass-covered hills, pine woods and meadows filled with flowers where time seemed to stand still.

The modern Russian city of Kaliningrad today gives little away about its past. It is difficult for the present-day visitor to imagine that before the Second World War it was Königsberg, the capital city of East Prussia, and was one of Germany's major centres of business, trade, culture and the arts. The same fresh and salty sea breezes blow in from the Baltic as they always did – Königsbergers claimed that theirs was the best air in Europe – but the few buildings which remain from before the war are an incongruous sight amongst the ugliness of the Stalinist architecture which overshadows them. Impressive merchant houses, churches, banks, theatres and museums once dominated the city centre and beyond the defensive walls, which formed a green girdle around the city, were residential suburbs of broad boulevards and substantial villas. These were the homes of the prosperous middle-class citizens, whilst the country mansions and huge estates of the East Prussian landed gentry dominated the surrounding countryside.

Königsberg was a frontier town on the extreme edge of Germany, and its walls, ditches and fourteen medieval bastions were built to fend off the Slavs who always pressed against Prussia's frontiers. In 1251 the Teutonic Knights[7] entered the northern Baltic province of Mazovia ostensibly to help protect it from attacks by the pagan Pruzzi who dominated the Eastern Baltic. They carried out their task with great brutality; thousands of Pruzzi were slaughtered, others were exiled and those who survived had Christianity forced upon them.[8] Four years later the Knights established a fortress on a small hill, 600 kilometres east of Berlin and a few kilometres inland from the Baltic Sea, on the marshy northern shores of the River Pregel. They drained the surrounding land and began the construction of a defensive wall around the city which was strengthened several times in the following centuries. They established a castle and named the new settlement Königsberg (King's Hill), after their ally, the King of Bohemia. Wooden houses and wharves soon clustered along the river banks and a massive brick cathedral was founded in 1333. In 1457 the Grand Master of the Teutonic Knights was forced to flee from his Marienburg fortress near Danzig and he took up residence in Königsberg Castle. In 1618 Prussia was joined by marriage with the state of Brandenburg and the provinces were united in 1660. Elector Frederick William III Brandenburg, was crowned King Frederick I of Prussia in 1701 and William I, who was to become the first modern emperor of all Germany in 1871, was crowned King of Prussia in the Castle church in 1861.[9]

The Castle was built on a small hill and dominated the city skyline. The tallest tower, the Spitzturm, was ninety metres high, from which (after climbing the 284 steps) there were magnificent views over the city. There were also four bay towers which surrounded a huge open courtyard in the heart of the Castle. Twice a day, in a custom which lasted from the sixteenth century to the Second World War, a wind band clambered to the top of one of the towers to play a morning and evening greeting. The evening chorale '*Nun ruhen alle Walder*'[10] – 'Now all the forests fall silent' – was a daily reminder of the city's peaceful setting, close to the East Prussian countryside. By the late nineteenth century the Castle was not just a military establishment but had also become a centre of entertainment and relaxation. Each summer weekend there were open-air band concerts, and the basement of the Blutgericht Tower, the Court of Blood, which had once been the torture chamber, had become the best known wine cellar in the whole of East Prussia. Königsbergers congregated there on Sunday afternoons to enjoy the sunshine and the wine, which was served from large beautifully carved and decorated barrels, or to drink coffee in one of the many cafés at the foot of the Castle walls.[11] These adjoined the gardens and promenades which ran alongside the green waters of the Schlossteich – Castle Lake – a long and picturesque ornamental lake dividing a large part of the northern half of the town. Originally built by the Knights to drain the marshy banks of the Pregel, the Schlossteich had become a peaceful oasis in the heart of the town and was the centre of the social life of a city. It was used for bathing and boating in the summer and for skating in winter. Many who grew up in Königsberg before the war remember this part of the city with great affection and recall that the sun always seemed to be shining.[12]

The first of the famous 'seven bridges of Königsberg'[13] to be constructed were the Kramer Brücke and the Grüne Brücke, linking the original Altstadt (Old Town) with the Kneiphof Island in the middle of the River Pregel.

Although Königsberg was both a naval and military stronghold into the twentieth century (Kaiser Wilhelm II came with great ceremony to inspect the troops in 1910) it owed its status from earlier times chiefly to the protected position of its harbour and its membership of the Hanseatic League[14] which made it one of the most important trading cities of the Baltic. The League, which thrived until the seventeenth century, traded in the major products of the Eastern Baltic and Königsberg prospered after it became a member in 1340. The city became a flourishing centre of commerce. It dealt in grain, wood, cereals, furs, honey, wax and amber, known locally as 'the gold of the sea', which was found in great abundance along the coast. By the early eighteenth century Königsberg was the second largest city in Prussia and by the time it reached the height of its prosperity in the nineteenth century it was the seventeenth largest town in the German Empire. Shipbuilding, printing, railway engineering and textile manufacturing all flourished and its docks handled more grain and wood than any other port in Germany. The palatial, light-blue-painted Stock Exchange, with its Renaissance-style façade, which is still standing, was built in the 1870s, and was the focal point of trade and finance as well as being one of the finest buildings in the city.

By then Königsberg was the cultural and economic centre of the region, boasted the largest book shop in Germany, claimed to manufacture the finest marzipan in the land and was at the forefront of technological advance. The railway came in 1853, linking the city to Berlin, Danzig, Dresden and Leipzig. In the 1860s the line was extended to St Petersburg and a new South Station was built, initially to serve new lines going to the coast but later linking Königsberg with Odessa and allowing goods to be transported from the Baltic to the Black Sea.[15] In 1895 the first electric trams in the whole of Germany replaced the old horse-drawn buses.

The inland lagoon, the Frisches Haff, which lay between Königsberg and the seaport of Pillau was shallow and for most of the town's history cargo had been transferred from sea-going merchant ships into low barges at Pillau, whilst in winter goods had to be transported by sledge. With Königsberg's increasing affluence, plans were made in 1878 to cut a sea canal from Pillau to Königsberg across the Frisches Haff. This was eventually opened in 1901 and it was kept ice-free in the winter with ice breakers. The opening of the sea canal led to an enormous expansion in the modern dockside area of the city, which had always been the centre of commercial activity, and it soon overwhelmed the old Speicherviertel, the medieval dock area, with its traditional tall timber-framed wharf houses each of which had their own name and sign, such as *Jonas mit der Walfisch* (Jonah and the Whale) and *Sonne* (Sun). Nevertheless, the older wharves still bustled with ships and sailors in the 1920s and the people of Königsberg enjoyed visiting the many inns around the old harbour

The River Pregel divided into two streams in the city centre around the densely built-up Kneiphof Island. Its narrow medieval streets were packed with shops and these and the workshops of craftsmen crowded around both the imposing brick Gothic cathedral and the original fine buildings of the Albertina University, founded in 1544 by Albert I, Duke of Prussia, as a German-speaking Lutheran place of learning. A memorial to Königsberg's most famous university teacher, the philosopher Immanuel Kant, who was born in the city in 1724, was on the north side of the Cathedral. Kant, who became one of the most significant of all the eighteenth-century philosophers, lived and worked in Königsberg all his life. Such was his influence that, when he died in 1804, the streets of the city were lined with people who had come to see his cortège pass. The essence of Kant's belief was that morality and human good lie inside all humans and reveal themselves in good will founded on universal moral laws. These laws oblige us to treat other human beings with respect. On his memorial, which still stands just outside the cathedral walls, are words which encapsulated the core of Kant's beliefs: *'Der bestirnte Himmel über mir, das moralische Gesetz in mir'* – 'The starry heavens above me, the moral law within me'.[16] They served this traditionally tolerant city well for nearly 200 years and it was to Königsberg's shame that the reputation for liberalism and fairness for which it was famed in the eighteenth and nineteenth centuries was overlooked by many in the years after the First World War.

The East Prussian countryside pressed against the city boundaries and farmers' wives, dressed in voluminous long skirts, aprons and shawls came in every day with baskets of blueberries, eggs and hand-made cheese and butter to the seven market squares in the town. Each market had its own specialities. At the Rossgärter market farmers sold live rabbits, chickens, pigeons, geese and ducks, and sellers called out to passers-by in the local *Plattdeutsch* dialect. One of the best sellers was tripe (known as *Kuddeln* in the local dialect) which was the main ingredient of a dish called *Fleck*. Men loved to eat this local speciality, often sold at the bars by the dockside – the so-called *Fleklokalen* – but their wives were not so keen. The tripe had to be cooked for five hours in a mixture of herbs and vinegar – and it was impossible to escape the smell! Country women from Lithuania came to sell vegetables at the Kohlmarkt on the south side of the river and fishwives sold freshwater and sea fish, all locally caught, from water-filled barrels at the Upper and Lower Fish Markets by the Pregel.[17]

Herring and cod were the most plentiful of the sea fish and hungry shoppers could eat another local speciality, grilled eel with mashed potatoes and sour cherry sauce. Purchases in the market were followed by an orgy of bottling and pickling. The people of Königsberg were thrifty and self-sufficient and most households had a cellar or store room in which there were rows of bottled beans, tomatoes, carrots, peas, cherries, strawberries, gooseberries, red- and black-currants, plums, fruit syrups, pickled gherkins and pickled cabbage. In normal times these were used in the long, hard East Prussian winters when the temperatures often fell below freezing for weeks and little was on sale in the markets except potatoes, red and white cabbage, carrots, onions, swedes and turnips. The plentiful produce and the skills of the housewives meant that the people of East Prussia and Königsberg were much better placed than most Germans to survive the deprivations of the two world wars.

The winters were cold and the River Pregel often remained ice-bound well into March. Christmas was therefore always a welcome respite and the first Christmas trees of the year appeared in early December in the Münzplatz, in front of the University, and in the Kaiser Wilhelm Platz. As in many other German cities, the Königsberg Christmas markets were a winter highlight. They were held in the Altstadt Market, the Rossgärter Market, the indoor market and on the Paradeplatz. The two biggest marzipan makers in Königsberg, Schwermer and Gelhaar, tempted shoppers with their beautifully wrapped marzipan sweets in the form of fruit, flowers and vegetables. There was a speciality called *Randmarzipan* packed in heart-shaped boxes, and marzipan models of the Castle decorated with candied fruit. Christmas trees were on sale and young boys would offer to carry them home for five or ten Pfennigs. The people of Königsberg were always well prepared for the cold at this time of the year. Wrapped up against the biting Baltic winds, they wore fur coats, overboots, mitts, and caps or scarves, pulled down over head and ears. The market women wrapped themselves in layers of skirts, shawls and scarves and beat their hands across their chests to keep warm. Housewives bought ingredients from their stalls for a Christmas speciality, *Schwarzsauer*, a black pudding served with dumplings made from the giblets of the Christmas day goose and dried fruit, together with lemon peel, sugar, spices, vinegar and goose blood.

The nineteenth century was a period of great prosperity for Königsberg but the outbreak of the First World War marked the beginning of thirty years of problems. East Prussia was the scene of great battles between German and Russian troops and, although the city did not come under direct attack, the Battles of Tannenberg and the Masurian Lakes took place near enough for it to be used as a military relief and hospital centre. Russia's decision to seek an armistice early in 1918 moved the main theatre of war to the Western Front, but the end of the war and the subsequent peace treaty left East Prussia and Königsberg isolated from the rest of Germany.

Chapter Two

THE SHAMEFUL PEACE

In the 1920s East Prussia was engulfed by a feeling of
terrible malaise, fuelled by deep resentment at the
manner in which this distant corner of Germany had been
treated by the 1919 Versailles Treaty at the end of the First
World War. In the autumn of 1918 the German armies were in
retreat and the social and economic fabric of the Kaiser's
Germany was disintegrating. The Kaiser abdicated on 9
November and the republican government had no alternative
but to sue for peace. The armistice of 11 November saved
Germany from invasion and military humiliation but also gave
rise to the myth that the country had not been defeated.
When the troops returned to Germany they were greeted as
heroes; returning soldiers were given a 'festive welcome',
writes Richard Bessel, and were greeted as men who had:

> . . . stood their ground undefeated up to the last
> minute . . . The inability to confront the fact that
> Germany's soldiers had been defeated on the
> battlefield left a damaging political legacy for
> Germany's first democracy.[1]

It was undoubtedly because of this that Germans convinced themselves that the peace treaty would deal with them lightly. When the terms were eventually presented to the German government in 1919 they were greeted with outrage. Germany was forced to accept complete responsibility for both the start of the Great War and the destruction caused by the fighting. Germany was to pay reparations of £6,600 million for the damage suffered by the Allies in the war. Austria was forbidden to unite with Germany and Germany's armed forces were to be severely cut. The German Army was restricted to 100,000 men and was prohibited from having tanks or military aircraft. The German Navy would not be permitted to build or operate submarines and was limited to only six obsolete battleships. The provinces of Alsace and Lorraine were handed back to France and the Saarland was to be administered by the League of Nations for the next fifteen years. The Rhineland was to be occupied by Allied troops and all German military installations and troops were banned from the territory.

For the East Prussians, the most serious territorial decision was that Germany should lose parts of West Prussia and Pomerania to Poland. One and a half million Germans were put under Polish rule and East Prussia was separated from the rest of Germany by the Polish Corridor. Part of the province of Silesia was given to Poland and the province of Memel was put under French control. No discussion of the terms of the treaty was permitted and the Germans were threatened with a renewed declaration of war if they did not sign what many regarded as 'the shameful peace' (*Schmachfrieden*). The treaty was signed in the Hall of Mirrors at Versailles on 28 June 1919, the anniversary of the murder of the Archduke Franz Ferdinand. The politicians who signed the treaty on Germany's behalf were, in many German eyes, the 'November criminals' who had 'stabbed Germany in the back' and the place and date of the signing produced in Germany a sense of enormous humiliation

It was commonly believed in East Prussia that no state suffered as much from the Versailles Peace Treaty as their own.[2] It lost large tracts of lands and was severed from West Prussia by the terms of the treaty. The pre-1918 population of West Prussia was an ethnic mix. The towns along the shores of the Baltic were mainly German and the aristocratic landowners were also German whilst the banks of the River Vistula, flowing north-west from Warsaw to Danzig, were principally inhabited by ethnic Poles. East Prussia itself was predominantly German.

The makers of the 1919 treaty wanted to re-create an independent Poland, out of territories which before 1914 had been German, Russian and Austrian. The peacemakers did not want to leave too many Germans or Poles in the 'wrong' country so this was to be done on ethnic lines. However, their deliberations were complicated by the wish to give Poland access to the Baltic Sea and the desire to make it possible for Poland to defend itself against Russia or Germany. In the end, they decided to give the new Poland access to the Baltic Sea by creating a Polish Corridor along the northern stretches of the River Vistula to Danzig, thus cutting East Prussia off from the rest of Germany. The new Poland would also include the largely Polish-speaking lands around Posen which had been part of West Prussia before the First World War.

Danzig, although originally a Polish settlement, was a largely German-populated city and its loss, the 'open wound in the East' as it came to be known to most Germans, was a terrible blow to German pride. Together with its hinterland, Danzig was to become a Free City under League of Nations control. A General Commissioner of the Republic of Poland in Danzig would represent the rights of Poland, and a Polish-dominated Senate would from then on run the city. Danzig had been one of the greatest ports on the Baltic Sea; it was famous for its amber, its goldsmiths and its clockmakers and was the birthplace of Daniel Fahrenheit and the philosopher Artur Schopenhauer. The city had particularly flourished in the nineteenth century, when it reverted to German rule after the end of the Napoleonic Wars, and its docks had been greatly extended. Many German-speakers lived in Danzig itself, although most of the peasant farmers who supplied the city with food from the surrounding countryside were Poles.

Despite the fact that they were in the minority in the city of Danzig, the Poles were given control of the customs service and the post office and were allowed to build a military garrison in a district known as the Westerplatte, a long spit of land protecting the entry to Danzig harbour. They also built a harbour at the neighbouring fishing village of Gdynia (Gotenhafen in German), twenty kilometres north of Danzig, with the help of the French. Danzig had once been one of the foremost ports in the Baltic but now the customs barriers against Germany imposed at the end of the war meant that trade dried up whilst Gdynia flourished.

In 1919 Danzig, the former capital of West Prussia, was a picturesque city with one of the finest surviving medieval districts in North Germany. Long, narrow streets lined with tall, richly decorated gabled merchant houses led down to the port where ships lay at anchor in the estuary of the Vistula. The quaint cobbled waterfront was lined with old shops, inns and counting houses.[3] The loss of the city was bitterly resented and in an effort to retain a foothold, the Weimar Republic called on the German inhabitants to remain there and to keep a grip on what was rightfully theirs. 'Poland's existence is unbearable', General Hans von Seeckt (head of the Germany Army during the Weimar Republic) wrote. 'It must disappear; Germany and Russia must re-establish the frontiers of 1914.'

Sybil Bannister moved to Danzig in 1935 with her German husband, Kurt Falkenberg, and she found the Germans who lived there 'morose, suspicious and unreliable', but she also realised that they were 'living in an atmosphere of fear and mistrust'.[4] They resented their isolation and, although they were not badly treated by the Poles, they had little in common with them and did not associate with them. They found it quite hard to make a living and were anxious that their own families did not stay in the city. There were German schools and they were allowed to speak German but plays and operas were always in Polish and the ethnic Germans were keen to send their sons away to German universities and to encourage them to stay there after they had graduated.

East Prussia remained German but it was isolated from the rest of Germany by the Polish Corridor. The only concession was that the part of Poland nearest to East Prussia, Marienwerder, around Allenstein should be allowed to vote on its future in a plebiscite. This was held in 1920 and an overwhelming majority of the population (97.9 per cent), which was predominantly German-speaking, voted to remain East Prussian. This had the effect of reducing the size of the Polish Corridor and it left one of the railway lines from Danzig to Warsaw under German control.

Trains from Germany were locked, by international law, whilst going through the Polish Corridor and passengers were not allowed to alight at Danzig. Instead they had to travel to Marienburg, the site of the largest Teutonic castle in Europe, to the south-east of Danzig, and change trains in order to travel back to Danzig. Tickets for these trains had to be paid for in Polish currency and the ticket collectors would not speak German to passengers. The window curtains in first- and second-class compartments had to be kept closed throughout the crossing of the Corridor and passengers frequently had to alight to have their passports checked by the Polish authorities. Marion von Dönhoff remembers how childhood visits by train to Berlin were regarded as adventurous undertakings and how on these occasions her family always said they were 'going to the Reich' whilst going home was a 'return to the province'.[5] Visitors who came to East Prussia from western Germany also always said that they had come from the Reich, having endured the travails of crossing the Corridor. The 'amputation', as the East Prussians called it, from the rest of Germany was a running sore which was to infect Germany throughout the next two decades.

Refusing to accept any responsibility for the First World War, neither Germany nor isolated East Prussia could come to terms with these humiliations or with the loss of parts of West Prussia, the Polish Corridor and Upper Silesia. The cession of these territories was both a terrible blow and a humiliation. Further north Memel (and with it half the Kurisches Nehrung) which claimed to be the oldest East Prussian city, had also been cut off from East Prussia. Germans made up eighty per cent of the population of the city, although the peasants who lived in the surrounding countryside were Lithuanian. The Treaty of Versailles decreed that Memel and the district around it should be ruled by a French administration under League of Nations mandate, but in 1923 the minority Memel Lithuanians, supported by Lithuanian troops, took over the city and forced the French out. This transfer of authority was internationally recognised but the German community there remained unhappy with their status and grew increasingly restive.

Königsberg was the German city nearest to what was now the Communist USSR, and with only Poland and Lithuania acting as a barrier, the conservative and capitalist citizens felt particularly vulnerable. As in many other parts of Germany, there were uprisings soon after the war ended as Communist sympathisers attempted to push Germany politically to the left. On 4 March 1919 there was a violent confrontation between demobbed soldiers who had joined a Freikorps unit,[6] the Gertschen Jäger, and 1,000 naval recruits wearing Communist red armbands. The Freikorps men crushed the demonstration, much to the relief of the city authorities whose sympathies were decidedly anti-Communist, but in the course of the confrontation forty-eight people died, including twenty-six civilians.

Twelve months later many Königsberg citizens publicly made known their support for Dr Wolfgang Kapp, leader of the so-called Kapp Putsch. Kapp was an official in the East Prussian civil service who marched into Berlin in 1920 with an army of Freikorps supporters in an attempt to overthrow the Weimar Government.[7] Kapp was a well-known figure in Königsberg: in 1915 he had thrown a great party in the town's fine Stock Exchange building to celebrate the hundredth anniversary of the birth of Bismarck and in 1917 he founded the German Fatherland Party in the city. The Kapp Putsch failed, but in Königsberg many workers came out on strike in support. Soon after this event Field Marshal von Hindenburg, one of Germany's leading soldiers of World War I and President of Germany 1925–34, was made an honorary freeman of the city and was given an honorary degree by the University, so it is perhaps not surprising that despite the part played by the Freikorps in Kapp's failed coup, they were not broken up. Instead, Freikorps units were used to defend the frontiers of East Prussia against Polish encroachment and to patrol Upper Silesia after the plebiscite of 1921 when the Poles revolted against the decision by the people of Silesia to remain German, 717,122 votes being cast for Germany against 483,514 for Poland.

Despite its problems in the 1920s, Königsberg outwardly retained its appearance of solid affluence and respectability, aided by the sterling efforts of its mayor, Hans Lohmeyer, and his deputy, Karl Gördeler. But its economic prosperity almost inevitably declined. With the loss of Danzig and Memel in 1919, the city became the only significant German port in the eastern Baltic and, as its export markets diminished in number and its volume of exports fell by two-thirds, unemployment began to rise.

To help alleviate these problems Lohmeyer and Gördeler built a new glass-roofed building for the Hauptbahnhof (the main [south] station), and a two-storey rotating road and railway bridge across the River Pregel, the Reichsbahn Brücke. To enhance trading opportunities a new shipping route was opened to Lübeck, the sea canal across the Haff was dredged to eight metres deep and Lohmeyer was the driving force behind the construction of a new airport on the site of the Devauer Feld, the old exercise yard of the Königsberg garrison, to establish better communications with Berlin, Stockholm, Riga and Moscow.[8] They began a programme of new house building and tramways in the suburbs; a new drama theatre was opened in 1927; and the famous city zoo, founded in 1896, was also rebuilt in the 1920s. It remained a major attraction for visitors to Königsberg throughout the Second World War. In order to encourage trade to the town, Lohmeyer and Gördeler established an annual trade fair with 2,000 stands, the *Ostmesse*, which attracted a substantial number of exhibitors every year between 1920 and 1943. (The site used for the *Ostmesse* was also later to be used as a centre for political rallies by the Nazis.) Nevertheless, the creation of the Polish Corridor seriously damaged export markets and the middle classes were badly affected both by the hyperinflation of 1923 and the economic effects of the Depression of the early 1930s.

Chapter Three

VOTING FOR THE NAZIS

Rural East Prussia was almost entirely dependent on agriculture. For most of its history it had been a land of large estates and semi-feudal peasant workers, largely self-sufficient, who lived on the produce of the fields and the abundant game which inhabited its vast forests. Although visitors loved what appeared to be a rural idyll and spoke fondly of 'the fertile brown of the earth, the golden yellow of the rolling wheat fields, the dark green of the endless woods and the shining silver of the thousand lakes',[1] the reality was that economically the whole area lagged behind the rest of Germany. In 1933, more than half the gainful employment in East Prussia was in agriculture and forestry, compared with twenty-nine per cent in the rest of Germany. In the mid-1920s the 2.5 million people of the province mostly earned their living from the land.

The creation of the Polish Corridor had effectively turned East Prussia into an economic island wedged between Poland, Russia and Lithuania. The effect on the already fragile state of agriculture was disastrous. Trade with the new neighbours was politically difficult. Russia had sunk into economic chaos following the Revolution and the Civil War and the Poles insisted that tariffs should be paid on goods transported on the railways that crossed their land to the rest of Germany. Profitability was reduced and there was a significant fall in the amount of grain, flour, butter, cheese and meat exported to the industrial areas of Germany.

Even before the First World War economic conditions had been difficult in much of East Prussia. The density of population in 1910 was 55 per square kilometre – the lowest in the Reich. Apart from in Königsberg itself, industrialisation had been slow to take hold and long before 1914 the disadvantages of a one-sided economy were already all too apparent. The First World War then did considerable damage to the rural economy of East Prussia. The government understandably gave priority to the war effort and farmers experienced shortages of fertiliser and machinery parts as well as losing young men and horses to the army. The government's need to provide the cities with affordable supplies of food in order to hold down wage demands necessitated a system of requisitions and price controls known as the Controlled Economy (*Zwangswirtschaft*). The price paid for the grain of East Prussia was so low that many farmers refused to sell to the government, preferring to hoard it and then sell it on the black market. Between 1871 and 1933 the province lost nearly a million inhabitants, most of whom moved to the industrialised towns of central and western Germany in the years after the First World War. In the mid-1930s, out of 4,805 parishes in East Prussia, 4,719 had populations of less than 2,000. Although Königsberg had a population of 336,000 in the 1920s, that of other important towns was small – Allenstein had 50,000 inhabitants, Elbing, 86,000, Insterburg 43,000 and Tilsit, 57,000.

Marion von Dönhoff recalls the extreme poverty in the years after the First World War. Poor workers from Königsberg were forced to come out into the countryside to collect discarded corn ears to take home to grind into flour. In the village near the castle of Friedrichstein where she lived, the villagers wore clogs on working days, preserving their only shoes for church on Sunday, after which they were carried home by hand to protect them from damage.[2]

Large landowners like the Dönhoffs faced financial ruin in the 1920s. These aristocratic families, the *Junker*, had always been 'threadbare nobility', precariously eking out a living from large estates which had never earned much money. They had survived because they had been artificially supported for over fifty years by a combination of tariff protection, direct subsidies from the state and cheap labour. The *Junker* families were conservative, independent-minded and very jealous of their way of life. Having refused to modernise before the First World War, they were now deeply in debt and unable to cope with the economic problems which resulted from East Prussia's isolation from the rest of Germany.

The Weimar government's priority was to continue and extend the compulsory measures, the *Zwangswirtschaft*, which had been put in place during the Great War. Agricultural producers saw this as an attack on the interests of rural Germany on behalf of more prosperous urban dwellers. Farmers had looked forward to a return to a free market but instead government controls remained in place until 1923; as a result the retention of *Zwangswirtschaft* led to bitter hostility between town and country and between farmers and government. The first post-war Social Democratic governments were well aware of this, but the continuation of the Allied blockade until 1919, coupled with the loss of fifteen per cent of Germany's agricultural land in the Versailles settlement, meant that they could see no alternative to the maintenance of controls. The situation for East Prussian farmers was also worsened by the existence of the Polish Corridor which made it extremely difficult for them to export their goods to the rest of the country.

In 1922, help was offered to the farmers of East Prussia through a subsidy, but the following year hyperinflation caused many bankruptcies, even though those with debts were able to wipe them out as the value of the mark collapsed. A rise in interest rates after the currency was stabilised in 1924 once more hit farmers hard. Many of them depended on loans to meet daily production costs and they could not avoid borrowing. Between the currency stabilisation and the onset of the economic crisis in 1929 agricultural debt rose by thirty-five per cent. In addition East Prussian farmers were affected by changing consumer tastes which led to tumbling potato and rye prices. In 1926 the provincial government decided it was impossible to demand taxes from East Prussian farmers.

In 1928, with agricultural income per capita at forty-four per cent below the national average, the Weimar government was forced to offer what became known as *Osthilfe* (literally 'east help' – subsidies to maintain the eastern provinces) to alleviate the problems of East Prussian farmers. The main recipients of this help were the owners of the large estates who dominated agriculture in the region; over 39 per cent of all the farmed land was in the hands of landowners who held farms of at least 100 hectares, compared with 20 per cent in the rest of Germany. In 9 out of the 37 administrative districts of East Prussia between 50 per cent and 68 per cent of farm land was in the hands of large landowners and in 1925 half of all land under cultivation was in the hands of 1.9 per cent of landowners. *Osthilfe* provided money to protect large estates on the verge of bankruptcy from foreclosure but did nothing to help with the high interest rates, which were the root of the problem.[3]

The political inclinations of East Prussian landowners and tenant farmers had always veered towards the right. Most did not support the Weimar Republic, and many were supporters of the DNVP (German National People's Party) which represented mainly agricultural interests, had an anti-socialist, anti-republican agenda, and believed in 'Christian values and German family life'. The party, which had strong support in Prussia, had vigorously opposed *Zwangswirtschaft*, was a strong supporter of agricultural subsidies and in 1929 opposed the Young Plan. This plan, financed by the USA, substantially reduced the reparations which Germany would have to pay as part of the Versailles settlement, and promised a quick restoration of the Rhineland. The intention of the plan was to reduce the financial burden on the Weimar government but the DNVP and other right-wing parties seized on the opportunity to revive the whole debate on Versailles and the question of German war guilt. This group of radical right supporters together formed a national committee calling for a plebiscite to reject the Young Plan calling it a 'death penalty' on the unborn and 'the Golgotha' of the German people.

The Nazi Party was quick to jump on the bandwagon and its successful propaganda campaign brought it rich rewards. In the 1929 election the Nazis scored their first considerable election success at the polls in East Prussia, mainly at the expense of the DNVP, basing their campaign on opposition to successive Weimar governments and offering programmes which varied according to the audience. The rural voters were promised an end to the 'senseless agricultural policy conducted by the regime and the parties in the interests of stock market capital'. The result of this had been, the Nazis declared, that 'the farmer sinks day by day into deeper debt and misery and in the end will be driven from his hearth and home while international money and Jewish capital take possession of his land.'[4]

Former inhabitants of East Prussia are in no doubt that Nazism was not a Prussian creation; they are quick to point out that at first the Nazi Party was treated with 'suspicion and mistrust' and that none of the leading figures in the Party were East Prussians.[5] Although subsequently Stalin was to blame Nazism on Prussia, many of the *Junker* class in fact looked down on Adolf Hitler and regarded him as a political upstart. Nevertheless, the failure of the DNVP to produce much in the way of tangible benefits for the agrarian interest led many East Prussians to consider switching allegiance to the Nazis. Hitler's anti-Communist stance and his intentions to restore West Prussia and Danzig to Germany, to get rid of the Polish Corridor, and to reclaim Memel were welcomed both by large landowners and the radical small-scale farmers who lived on the southern borders of the province. Then the world economic crisis, which began in October 1929 following the collapse of share prices on Wall Street, made the situation of East Prussian farmers even worse than before. The indebtedness of farmers which, as we have seen, had been rising rapidly throughout the 1920s, coupled with the onset of the Depression, caused their financial situation to worsen swiftly as agricultural prices and sales collapsed. Neither peasants nor landowners could find the money to repay their debts. The effect of the calamity on the German people was profound and, in the view of Joachim Fest, 'an overwhelming psychological crisis' descended on the country which 'destroyed all political, moral and intellectual standards', and made the people turn to anyone who offered hope.

It was the opportunity Hitler needed to make his political mark. His National Socialist Party had struggled to gain significant support in the 1920s but the severe rise in unemployment which now took place gave him the opening he had been waiting for. He geared himself up to take full advantage of the Weimar government's economic difficulties Alan Bullock, in *Hitler: A Study in Tyranny*, urges his readers to translate the unemployment figures:

. . . into terms of men standing hopelessly on the street corners of every industrial town in Germany; of houses without food or warmth; of boys and girls leaving school without any chance of a job, and one may begin to guess something of the incalculable human anxiety and bitterness burned into the minds of millions of ordinary German working men and women.[6]

Hitler wrote in the Nazi press:

Never in my life have I been so well disposed and inwardly contented as in these days. For hard reality has opened the eyes of millions of Germans to the unprecedented swindles, lies and betrayals of the Marxist deceivers of the people.[7]

Nazi mass rallies took place and Party propaganda flooded Germany.

Unemployment figures had been rising relentlessly since the start of the Depression in 1929 when they had stood at 1,320,000. By September 1930 they had increased to 3 million, and a year later they reached over 4.25 million. In September 1932 over 5 million were unemployed and the 6 million figure was reached in January 1933. These stark figures do not reflect the terrible human suffering which lay behind them; nearly half of all German families were affected by unemployment and for most of the unemployed there was little chance of a job. With their poverty came the fear of homelessness; unsympathetic landlords repossessed houses and flats when the rent was not paid and families were forced to move into the streets. A mood of pessimism seemed to grip the whole nation. The British Ambassador, returning to Berlin in July 1931, was 'much struck by the emptiness of the streets and the unnatural silence hanging over the city, and particularly by an atmosphere of extreme tension.'

In the early 1930s, many East Prussians were seduced by Nazi promises. *Osthilfe*, which still mainly benefited the big landowners of the region, had not succeeded in solving the problems of East Prussian farming and the agricultural policies of the Brüning government (1930–2) also did nothing to alleviate the worsening economic situation. The antipathy of the East Prussians to Brüning was further enhanced by plans he drew up in December 1932 which included the ending of agricultural quotas, which had been established for the benefit of large landowners, and the breaking up of some inefficient and bankrupt East Prussian estates in order to resettle over 600,000 unemployed on the land.

Landowners got wind of these proposals and, on 12 January 1933, the association of large farmers, the *Landbund*, bitterly attacked the government. Their spokesmen then visited the ageing President Hindenburg and persuaded him that Brüning was an 'agrarian Bolshevik' bent on the ruination of traditional agriculture.

Taking advantage of the situation, the Nazis, who had recently announced a policy on agriculture designed specifically to win the agricultural vote (signed personally by Hitler), now began to praise farmers as 'the backbone' of the economy; as a result the Nazis were increasingly regarded as the party to turn to. They promised state credits, reductions and remissions in taxes, and higher tariffs on imported goods.

The fundamentally right-wing East Prussians were also attracted by the impression created by the Nazis that they would return Germany to a state of order at a time when the traditional structures of the country seemed to be under increasing threat. Many who had previously regarded Hitler and his followers as vulgar were now seduced by the promises of Nazi politicians to reverse the follies of Weimar and were impressed by their single-minded determination to unravel the country's problems.

In 1928 the Nazi Party had gained only 0.8 per cent of the East Prussian vote but in September 1930 this rose to nineteen per cent. Nazi propaganda and the Party's anti-Marxist stand, as well as its promises to preserve agriculture, had proved enough to persuade voters that their problems, which they believed ultimately resulted from the isolation of their frontier province, would best be tackled by Hitler. The German diplomat and diarist Count Harry Kessler wrote on election day that it was:

> . . . a black day for Germany. National Socialism is a delirium of the German lower middle class. The poison of its disease may, however, bring down ruin on Germany and Europe for decades ahead.

Two weeks later he travelled from Berlin to Weimar:

> On our train there were crowds of SA members travelling to Coblenz for a 'liberation' ceremony, in a uniform hardly distinguishable from the Reichswehr. At Halle they were already bawling *The Watch on the Rhine* and other 'patriotic songs'. At Weimar they spread over the platform, down the stairs, into the waiting rooms. Snotty-nosed brats most of them. Drunk, too, with their tunics half unbuttoned, in a bickering, brawling mood, abusive to other passengers, utterly undisciplined.[8]

Support for the Nazis was significantly strengthened by fear of the Communists, who had their own plans for Germany. The Communist Party, the KPD, seemed young, dynamic and forceful and was attractive to intellectuals and artists who were inspired by Communist promises to create a new society and political system. With the start of the Depression, votes for the Communists increased sharply and the Party became particularly attractive to the young unskilled who had no jobs.

In the autumn of 1931 the Nazi Party submitted its own list of candidates for election to chambers of agriculture in Prussia. Only landowners were allowed to vote and the Party made a particularly strong showing in East Prussia. The humiliation of Versailles, the castration of the Army, the fear of Communism and continuing economic problems, combined with the Nazi promise to restore agriculture's place in the economy, resulted in the Nazi share of the vote in East Prussia in the general election of July 1932 increasing to 47.1 per cent.

Recent research indicates that in the elections of 1930, July 1932 and 1933 the Nazis had more success than any other party in gaining voters who had not cast a vote at the previous poll.[9] It is likely that the imprecise nature of the Nazi programme contributed to the Party's great triumphs. It appealed to radicals and conservatives, anti-socialists and nationalists, reactionaries and revolutionaries. Even more importantly it seemed attractive to all classes of society so that lower middle-class voters and tenant farmers of East Prussia were joined by the old land-owning *Junker* classes, who in the main were hostile to the multi-party democracy of the Weimar Republic. In January 1932 Hitler won over Germany's industrial leadership in a speech to the Industry Club of Düsseldorf in which he declared that Communism was the greatest danger to German nationalism. Hitler argued that liberal democracy and the idea of human equality would inevitably lead to communism:

> In periods of national decline we always find that in place of the value of personality there is substituted a levelling idea of the supremacy of mere numbers, democracy, [but now] the concept of human equality itself has been developed into a political and economic 'system' and this system . . . is Communism.[10]

A few months later prominent East Prussian estate owners helped to sabotage the Brüning and Schleicher governments and connived with Brüning's replacement as Chancellor, Franz von Papen, in persuading President Hindenburg to appoint Hitler as Chancellor on 30 January 1933, even though many of them regarded him with social disdain.

The Nazi Party immediately took charge of national radio stations. In Königsberg and throughout East Prussia, people listened to the broadcast from Berlin:

> Like a blazing fire [cried the announcer] the news spread across Germany. Adolf Hitler is Chancellor of the Reich. A million hearts are aflame. Rejoicing and gratitude pour forth . . . a procession of blazing torches is streaming up the Wilhelmstrasse. Their banners glow blood red. A glorious and inspiring sight![11]

After achieving power Hitler, through the Enabling Act of 23 March, became the dictator of Germany. Amongst a raft of measures the Nazis reassured the rural voters by fixing food prices and regulating commodity production in order to ensure a steady food supply and to shield growers from overseas competition. The underlying aim was to make Germany self-sufficient in food. As a result farm incomes improved for several years after the Nazi take-over and this was enough to keep rural discontent in East Prussia and other agricultural areas at manageable levels. Even so agriculture's share of Germany's GNP continued to decline, from just over twelve per cent in 1927 to less than ten per cent by 1939 and full self-sufficiency was not achieved. When war broke out in 1939 Germany had achieved eighty-three per cent self-sufficiency but was hard pressed to maintain this level of production as more and more labourers were conscripted into the armed forces.

Chapter Four

A FRESH BEGINNING

The first Königsberg citizen to join the Nazi Party was a master baker who visited Munich in the early 1920s and fell in with the fledgling Nazi Party. In 1925 a small Sturm Abteilung (SA – the Nazi Party 'storm-troops') group was formed in Königsberg itself, and was addressed so provocatively by Josef Goebbels, the Party propaganda chief, in 1926 that fighting broke out in the meeting room between opposing factions.[1] In 1928 when Erich Koch,[2] a man who became notorious for his treatment of the population of the Ukraine after the German invasion, was appointed Gauleiter (District Leader) of East Prussia by Hitler, there were just eighty Party members in the town. The Mayor of Königsberg, Dr Lohmeyer, recalled later how the plots against him had begun soon after Koch's arrival. Koch tried 'permanently to rub me up the wrong way,' he wrote, 'and when once I repelled him energetically he answered me back "When we come to power you will be one of the first to go." And so it turned out.'[3]

Koch set about organising the Nazis into an efficient party machine by establishing special groups of students, office workers and farmers. He founded a Nazi newspaper, the *Ostdeutscher Beobachter*, (which was renamed the *Preussische Zeitung* in 1931) and he tried to boost support by bringing Hitler to Königsberg in May 1929 to speak in the town hall.

A few months after Hitler's visit Wall Street crashed and so did the economy of Königsberg. Over 500 local firms went bankrupt in the course of a few months; unemployment rose sharply and by 1932 a quarter of the population was living on state hand-outs. Voters were increasingly inclined to turn to the extreme parties, the Communists and the Nazis, who were quick to take advantage of the situation. The German Communist Party had its own street-fighter force to intimidate political opponents and to protect its meetings. This Red Front Fighters' League engaged in bloody street battles with right-wing paramilitary units like the SA and distributed propaganda material; at times the streets of many German cities were taken over by these opposing mobs and people cowered in their homes and workplaces waiting for the violence to end. There were many thousands of unemployed in Königsberg in the early 1930s and they were restless and angry about the 'injustices' that had been done to them. They queued every day to collect their dole money and the queues often became an area of conflict between the Red Front and the SA. Swearing matches and brawls frequently broke out as worsening violence erupted between these two extreme factions.

The July elections of 1932 were accompanied by extreme violence in the city. On the night of 31 July/1 August massive disturbances took place with assassination attempts, arson and fire bombing. The police report for these nights records petrol stations on fire, break-ins at several city buildings, the attempted murder of the editor-in-chief of the *Volkszeitung* and the state president, and the assassination of a state official, Herr Sauf.

Early in 1933 there was a fierce clash between supporters of the National Socialists and the Red Front when streets in the Altstadt were thronged with rival gangs.[4] Next morning there were reports in the newspapers that a member of the SA, Fritz Tschierse, had been knifed to death. After the Nazi take-over, a bronze memorial was erected to him and on every public holiday goose-stepping Party members held a vigil, wreaths were laid and flares were burnt in memory of this Nazi Party martyr, and the Gesekus Platz in the Altstadt where he died was renamed Tschierse Strasse.

In 1933 Hitler came to Königsberg again, this time in triumph, to 'the ancient coronation town', on the eve of the Reichstag election, 5 March 1933 – a day he called 'the day of the awakening nation'. He made a pre-election broadcast to the people of Germany from the city on 4 March at the end of a month of torchlight processions, huge demonstrations, cheering crowds, blaring loudspeakers, mob oratory, streets hung with swastika flags. In his public speech to a rapturous crowd Hitler reminded the people that President Hindenburg had been responsible for liberating East Prussia from Russia in the First World War, and declared, 'We want to make a fresh beginning with the truth; the people must understand that its future lies only in its own strength.' In conclusion he urged them, 'Hold your heads up high and proud once again. Now you are no longer enslaved and unfree; now you are free again!'[5] All the wireless stations in Germany had been ordered to broadcast his words not just to people's homes but also on loudspeakers in the streets and SA columns were present in many places to give weight to the Führer's oratory.

Victor Klemperer wrote about the event in his diary:

> On Saturday the 4th, I heard a part of Hitler's speech
> from Königsberg. The front of a hotel at the railway

station, illuminated, a torchlight procession in front of
it, torchbearers and swastika flag bearers on the
balconies and loudspeakers. I understood only words.
But the tone! The unctuous bawling, truly bawling, of
a priest.[6]

As the speech ended, martial music blended with the sound
of the bells of Königsberg Cathedral and 'freedom bonfires'
blazed on the hilltops along what Hitler called the 'threatened
frontier of the east'. Wilhelm Matull went to cast his vote in
Königsberg on 5 March and found the place swarming with
SA. Helga Gerhardi also remembers the Königsberg people
who took part in the election that day. She was a child and
they voted, she thought, on whether they supported Hitler as
the new chancellor: 'The voting on that day was only to say
"Yes" or "No". If you said "Yes" you received a little pin with
"Ja" formed from wire, which was pinned to the lapel.' Her
impression was that 'Everybody seemed to have such a pin on
that day, although it was a secret ballot.'[7] Dora Skopp recalls,
however, that her parents were amongst those who did vote
'No' – but they were both given a 'Ja' pin, which went into the
rubbish bin when they got home.[8]

Although nationally the Nazis won just 44 per cent of the
votes cast on that day, 56.5 per cent of the East Prussian
electorate voted for the Nazis – the largest percentage in the
whole Reich. After this result Mayor Lohmeyer, was sacked.
Commentators on Königsberg itself have no doubt that the
mass meeting addressed by Hitler had a substantial effect on
the voting. In all 88,551 people voted for the Nazis compared
with 75,760 in the July 1932 election and 62, 880 in November
1932. (In 1928 just 2,000 citizens had voted for the Nazis.)[9]

On 10 May 1933 a book burning took place on the main
parade ground, the Trommelplatz, which included 'any book
which acts subversively on our future or strikes at the root of

German thought, the German home and the driving forces of our people.' Sixteen members of the University staff were sacked because of their political views or racial origins and two of the longest-serving school headmasters were dismissed. A new edict to the editors of newspapers in October 1933 set out new orders for the German press. All editors were required by law to be citizens of the Reich, to pledge to uphold the Nazi state and to exclude any material that might weaken the power of the German state. Many leading officials who had served Königsberg since the war were ejected from their posts if they were not Nazi Party members. There were numerous Party members who were willing to replace those who had been forced to leave.

Two of the most important Königsberg newspapers, the *Königsberger Zeitung* and the *Hartungsche Zeitung* appeared for the last time, having been banned by the Nazis. The SS seized and shut down the offices of the local Social Democratic Party, trade union offices and the Masonic lodge. As in other German cities, many old street names were changed – the Hansa Platz became Adolf Hitler Strasse, the Königsallee became Hermann Göring Strasse (it became Stalinallee in 1945) and other streets were renamed Erich Koch Platz and Horst Wessel Strasse. In July 1934 during 'The Night of the Long Knives' when Hitler turned on the SA and other opponents, several prominent Königsberg citizens were murdered by the SS, including the East Prussian President, Max von Bahrfeldt, town councillor Zirpens and Otto Wyrgatsch, editor-in-chief of the *Königsberger Zeitung*. Later that year several other leading citizens were seized by the SS and shot.

After the Nazi take-over Erich Koch made a firm promise that East Prussia would soon be free from unemployment. He made strenuous efforts to win support from Hitler for the East Prussian economy. His aim was to reduce the number of unemployed from 102,000 and he succeeded in bringing it down to 18,200 by 1935 by requesting an injection of money so that Königsberg workers could participate in the rearmament programme and the civil building programme. There is no doubt that after 1933 the economy of the town improved. The numbers employed in the docks, engineering and other industries increased, and employment benefited particularly from the building of more housing and the construction of an *Autobahn* from Königsberg to Elbing, although the planned extension to Danzig and Berlin was never started. The 1930s also saw the building of a kindergarten, a youth hostel, a mother and children's home and the restoration of several schools. Koch's policy was a definite success, notwithstanding the fact that he indulged in black-market operations which enhanced his own fortune considerably. The improvement in the economy increased support for the Party even though neither agriculture nor firms involved largely with the export trade revived as much as Koch had hoped.[10]

Marianne Mackinnon, who married a British soldier after the war, recalls hearing, as a child, a political broadcaster referring to Hitler as 'the Messiah of Germany'. When she asked her father what it meant he replied, 'someone who has come to liberate his people and his country'. A janitor's wife, Frau Klein, 'often spoke of Hitler as a godsend' and Herr Kahl the baker referred to the Führer as 'the right man who had come at the right time'. Marianne noticed social changes, too, particularly at her school. Some crept in subtly, others were introduced 'as though with trumpets and drums'. School began each day with the Hitler salute. Everyone was required to use it when they greeted someone in the street:

> Heil Hitler! The new greeting was a bore. Arm up,
> arm down, up, down. But it was the formal salute in

Germany now and everyone did as they were told, including my father.

Marianne's father had come home from work one day to tell the family that he had joined the Party. There was the offer of a directorship if he would join up. He had been told to 'think of the firm's political image' and in the end he had taken the oath in order to avoid demotion to sales clerk. At her school there were new textbooks, new songs, a new syllabus and new rules about writing in Gothic script, and physical education replaced religious instruction. Marianne's teacher, Frau Bienert, explained how Hitler wanted all children to have a healthy mind in a healthy body. The children liked this aspect of the new regime – an hour's sport each day was much better than lessons.[11]

In Marianne's school, as in all others in Germany, sport and discipline seemed to be the most important parts of the curriculum after Hitler came to power. Lessons became more and more politicised and pupils at the school, like thousands of others across the country in 1935, when the Saar plebiscite was taking place, were forced to recite a verse written in 1920 by Hanns Maria Lux:

Deutsch ist die Saar, Deutsch immerdar,
Deutsch ist das Lied und deutsch das Wort,
Und deutsch der Berge schwarzer Hort.

[The Saar is German, German forever,
The song is German and the language is German,
And so is the black treasure in the mountains.][12]

The people of the Upper Saar duly voted to rejoin Germany and this gave Hitler the justification he needed to retake the demilitarised Rhineland in 1936 and then to turn to Austria in 1938. Hitler's troops marched into Austria in

March 1938 and entered Vienna on the 12th to an enthusiastic reception from many of its people. The *Anschluss*, the union of Austria and Germany, took place despite diplomatic protests from Britain and France. Their complaints were not followed up by any military intervention and Hitler's confidence in his ability to carry out further expansion was fuelled still more. Thus Hitler was seen by many in Königsberg as a hero.

Two years earlier, in May 1936, the young Martin Bergau, who lived at the coastal resort of Palmnicken, had been with his school class to see the Führer on the way back from a visit Hitler had made to German-speaking Poland and Königsberg. At Palmnicken station, wagons were decorated with birch leaves and long planks were in place from which they would be able to see him. For Martin's class it was 'a great adventure' to be gathered with other school children amongst a crowd thrilled to see 'the beloved Führer'. As he passed by in his open-top limousine the crowd cheered this man who 'three years later was going to throw the world into chaos' and would sacrifice East Prussia and its people.[13]

Hitler came to Königsberg again on 25 March 1938, eleven days after the annexation of Austria. Preparations had been in progress for days and on the day of the visit the city was ablaze with Nazi flags and banners and the shops were filled with little flags with pictures of the Führer, the swastika and a decoration of oak and laurel leaves. Householders were instructed to hang at least one Nazi flag from their windows. Every fifty metres banners hung over the streets, the Hitler Youth and SS had practised their marches to perfection and bands played martial songs. Old women from the country sold bunches of violets to the people crammed along the pavements. All the school children of the city marched to the route in rows of six and took up positions along both sides of the road. Enthusiastic crowds lined the official route from the station to the Castle and they roared their support, raised their arms in the Nazi salute and threw the violets to Hitler as he passed by.

Observers remember the sense of intoxication that gripped the crowd. They enjoyed a great feeling of pride as they watched Hitler standing upright in his car, flanked by motor bikes, with his right hand raised in greeting.[14] He was on his way to the stadium, where he delivered a speech defending the annexation of Austria. His words were relayed around the town by loudspeakers as well as being broadcast to the nation. He had just called an election to gain public support for the annexation and in his speech he reassured his German followers. 'When I crossed the former frontier I was with a stream of love such as I have never experienced. We came not as tyrants but as liberators.'[15] The election was held on 10 April 1938 and resulted in a 99 per cent vote in favour.

On 23 March the next year local people were delighted when they learnt that the former East Prussian territory of Memel had been returned to the Reich, just a week after the Nazi occupation of Prague. Hitler had personally gone with the German Navy, on board the pocket battleship *Deutschland*, to oversee the 'recovery' of this small city on the northern frontier of East Prussia. Whilst on board he had a radio conversation with the Lithuanian government demanding to know whether he would be able to enter Memel peacefully or whether he would have to force his way in. With Foreign Minister Ribbentrop adding weight by threatening Lithuanian envoys who had been summoned to Berlin, the Lithuanians had bowed to Hitler's demands and turned the region over without a fight. The German Navy was off shore, ready to invade but was deprived of a chance to launch the planned assault. It was to be Hitler's last bloodless conquest.

Chapter Five

THE JEWS OF KÖNIGSBERG

Königsberg, which had a relatively small Jewish population, was the location Hitler chose to make a speech in August 1935 in which he told loyal Party members that anti-Jewish legislation was in preparation and would become a central aim of the government. These were the Nuremberg Laws, the Citizenship Law and the Law for the Protection of German Blood and Honour which passed into statute on 15 September 1935.

The first Jews had arrived in Königsberg in 1540; the last left in April 1948. The first synagogue in the town was constructed in 1756. At its peak in 1880, bolstered by refugees from *pogroms* in western Russia, the Jewish population was about 5,000 (3.6 per cent of the total population). By the time of the Nazi take-over in 1933, the Jewish population was about 3,200, served by two synagogues. There was a large synagogue on the Lindenstrasse, one of the city's main streets and, behind it in its back rooms, was the Jewish school. There was also a smaller synagogue, Adas Israel, in a residential area of the old city in the Seilerstrasse, which was attended by Orthodox Jews.

Although the rural population of East Prussia had always tended to be right-wing, the city of Königsberg was traditionally liberal and tolerant. Jewish students were admitted to the University in 1712 and the philosopher Immanuel Kant had a substantial number of Jewish pupils. In the early nineteenth century many of the Jewish immigrants from Russia lived in the town centre around the Lindenstrasse and the nearby Kaiserstrasse[1] but later the more prosperous moved out to the suburbs and became engaged in many aspects of commerce and business, supported the cultural life and played an increasing role in local politics.[2]

During the late nineteenth century the intellectual elite of the city frequented the salons of highly respected Jewish families, such as Friedlander and Herz, and the large new synagogue on Lindenstrasse was constructed in the 1890s with seating for 1,500 people. Like many synagogues built in Germany at this time it was, at fifty metres high, cathedral-like in its construction, and its gilded splendour reflected the growing wealth and contentment of the Jewish population. It was within sight of the Cathedral, which could be reached by crossing the wooden Hönig Brücke (Honey Bridge) on to the Kneiphof Island. It had an organ and a choir and the services were conducted in German, using the scriptural translations of the eighteenth-century Jewish writer and thinker, Moses Mendelssohn. The opening ceremony of the synagogue was attended by many civic dignitaries and the Mayor of Königsberg, Burgermeister Brinkmann, spoke of the goodwill that existed between the Christian and Jewish communities of the city and noted how people of all religions and confessions lived together in the town in peace and harmony

By the 1920s this harmony had faded as the province's isolation and increasing economic problems caused many to look for scapegoats. Urged on by both the SA and members of the Freikorps, anti-Semitism became rife in the city even before the Nazis came to power. In 1920 the city's police chief, Josef Lübbring, forbade the selling of anti-Semitic newspapers in the city, and in 1924 he managed to prevent Hitler from speaking in Königsberg. Yet, by then, many Jews felt threatened; the murder of the Jewish government minister Walter Rathenau[3] by right-wing extremists in Berlin on 24 June 1922 was keenly felt by many Jews in Königsberg, even though there was a large demonstration against the murder of Rathenau on the streets the next day. After the arrival of Erich Koch in 1928, when the Party did well in the city council elections, the police lost control over the spreading terror in the streets. Almost immediately the Nazis started to 'clean up the streets' by pouncing on Communists, Social Democrats and Jews. In Berlin in October 1930, diplomat Count Harry Kessler, who loathed the Nazis, witnessed events which were echoed in Königsberg and other cities:

> October 13. Reichstag opening. The whole afternoon and evening mass demonstrations by the Nazis. During the afternoon they smashed the windows of Wertheim Grünfelde and other department stores in the Leipzigerstrasse. In the evening they assembled in the Potsdamer Platz shouting 'Germany awake', 'Death to Judah', and 'Heil Hitler'. In the main they consisted of adolescent riff-raff who made off yelling as soon as the police began to use rubber truncheons. I have never witnessed so much rabble in these parts.[4]

In March 1932 Ludwig Goldstein, the Jewish editor of the Königsberg newspaper the *Hartungsche Zeitung*, was sacked and in the same month the Jewish proprietor of one of the cinemas was attacked and died three days later from his injuries. In April 1933, just over two months after Hitler came to power, Jews were banned from civil service jobs in Germany and he called for a boycott of all Jewish establishments. In Königsberg, encouraged by Erich Koch, malevolence towards the Jews now became particularly evident. There had been a systematic campaign of violence against the Jews from the day Hitler became Chancellor in January and by February 1933 over 500 had already left the city.[5]

Elsewhere in East Prussia, Jewish homes and shops were subjected to nightly attacks. Koch enforced the banning of Jewish families from shops and public places and put into practice the full extent of Nazi anti-Jewish legislation. There were many attacks on Jewish property, particularly on the many shops owned by Jewish families, and the people of Königsberg, who had so recently prided themselves on their tolerance, allowed themselves to be seduced by the prejudice and violence stirred up by the SA.

It became common for Jewish children to be ambushed and beaten up on their way home from school by gangs of Hitler Youth, who were fed on anti-Semitic propaganda. The slogan *'Juda Verrecke'* – 'Death to Jewry' – was scrawled on many buildings in the city and for Michael Wieck, a boy with a Jewish mother, Jew-baiting became part of his day-to-day experience. Often this took the form of odd remarks and little jokes about 'the haggling Jew' but such phrases dripped 'into the soul like concentrated acid'.[6]

Wieck was not really surprised one day in November 1938, when his mother told him he could not go to the Jewish school that day as the building in the Lindenstrasse had been attacked and the school had been burnt down. It was the morning after *Kristallnacht*, the 'Night of Broken Glass', when all over Germany a *pogrom* was launched against Jews following the assassination in Paris of Ernst von Rath, a junior diplomat, by a young Polish Jew, Herschel Grynzpan. Rath had studied in Königsberg and joined the Nazi Party there. Grynzpan's attack was described by Goebbels' propaganda machine as a conspiratorial attack by 'international Jewry' against the Reich and against the Führer himself.

On the night of 9/10 November, gangs of Nazi thugs roamed through Jewish neighbourhoods breaking windows of Jewish businesses and homes, burning synagogues and looting. In all at least 150 synagogues in Germany were destroyed and almost 7,500 Jewish businesses were ruined. Some 26,000 Jews were arrested and sent to concentration camps; other Jews were attacked and beaten and 91 died.

As a result of Grynzpan's connections with Königsberg, the attacks were particularly violent there; the attackers locked themselves inside the synagogue in the Lindenstrasse and desecrated the Torah scrolls, ripping them apart and throwing them into the street. The furniture of the Jewish orphanage next door was set on fire and the children ran out into the streets in panic. They did not have time to get dressed and stood shivering in their night clothes as they watched the attackers set fire to the synagogue's dome. Michael Wieck remembers how severely the synagogue was damaged. 'Only a few years later, Königsberg looked exactly like this, and if you wanted to you could see this as God's judgement.'[7] The Orthodox synagogue, Adas Israel, was also attacked but it was saved from destruction because of its position in the Seilerstrasse in the Altstadt. Its proximity to other properties meant that a fire in the synagogue would have done serious damage to neighbouring dwellings. In all 450 Jews were arrested during the night and the last head rabbi of Königsberg, Josef Dunner, left Königsberg on *Kristallnacht* after the synagogue had been set on fire.

Helga Gerhardi witnessed the effects of the attack on Stern, one of the largest stores in the town, which took place that night. It was a three-floor department store which had always been very popular with the townsfolk. On the morning of 10 November, when Helga arrived at school, she heard that the shop had been broken into. After lessons were over she went home via the town centre:

> The place looked awful. All the windows were broken and the building stared at me with great big holes. Everything was broken inside, counters, the display units, and all furniture. Paper, boxes, clothes, china, shoes, saucepans, cushions slit open, and feathers flying about . . . I heard remarks like 'They did it last night. Some of them left with armfuls of boxes, others with clothes, and even fur coats. It is not right to destroy things like that, but they are Jewish. Why don't they share the stuff out? There are plenty of poor people who would be glad of it.'[8]

Dora Skopp lived with her family in the middle of the Altstadt retail district above her father's fur shop. She was woken at 4.00 a.m. by the sound of breaking glass in the street below and in the twilight she saw men in brown uniforms destroying the interior of the lamp shop opposite. After they had broken the windows they began to loot, hiding things in their pockets and then running away. Her father went out and found his fur shop safe, but the porcelain shop next door had been destroyed and all those around owned by Jews had been smashed. The attackers had urinated on things they could not destroy. Hitler's supporters had also attacked Jewish-owned hotels and restaurants in the town and daubed them with the slogan '*Juden unerwünscht*' – 'Jews not welcome'. The Jewish cemetery had also been attacked.[9] Goebbels boasted that on *Kristallnacht* over 150 synagogues (the true figure was probably higher) were burned down and destroyed.

Eventually the Jewish children of Königsberg went back to school in the Jewish orphanage behind the large synagogue –

a building which survived until the end of the war. The ruined synagogue was left empty, a silent memorial to suffering, and the Jews who remained attended the Adas Israel synagogue. In 1942, Dora Skopp was returning from her school on the Kneiphof Island via the Hönig Brücke, which linked the Lindenstrasse to the Island. Her way was barred by four policemen, who said, 'The way is blocked, go back; leave the road.' She and her friends were pushed into a small side street but she crept back until she had a view of the Lindenstrasse. She could see that the remains of the synagogue had been on fire and that firemen were helping people out. No one knew what had happened but the firemen were doing all they could to rescue those who were trapped. Suddenly a siren sounded:

> The fire engines drew back, there was a loud crack
> and the cupola of the synagogue collapsed in a cloud
> of dust. Then the police opened the bridge again.
> After that I never saw the children marked with a star
> on the bridge again.[10]

She did not see the Jewish children again because they and their families had been ordered to the Königsberg North Station to await transportation. They trudged pitifully through the streets loaded down with bundles of possessions. They were a wretched sight, resembling, as Michael Wieck, records, 'only in outward appearance the streams of refugees that were later to pour out from bombed-out cities'. He recalls how the people of Königsberg watched passively, or turned away. The transport of the Jews had begun some months before and the people had, even then, 'chosen not to notice what they did not wish to see', but on this occasion so many people were expelled that he felt that, despite their passivity, 'There were many bad consciences in Königsberg that day.' The collection point was a large riding school and

SS men were standing at tables with papers and files. The place was crowded with Jewish families waiting to be processed, and when it was done they were taken to the station to be transported:

> ... perhaps to Chelmno, the concentration camp not so far from East Prussia in which they carried out their first gas chamber trials – or perhaps to Riga, or maybe even to Auschwitz.[11]

Helga Gerhardi recalls how the people of Königsberg were slowly:

> ... inspired, manipulated and seduced by National Socialism. We were taught at school that the Jews were the cause of all Germany's misfortunes. We had a small picture book in the school library in which were the words:
>
> Trau keinem Fuchs auf grüner Heid
> Und keinem Juden bei seinem Eid.
>
> [Trust not a fox out on the heath
> Nor a Jew giving his oath.][12]

Dora Skopp remembers a Good Friday church service in the Altstadt Church on the Paradeplatz when she was about ten when she first became aware of the conflict between Christian beliefs and the National Socialist propaganda she heard at school and in the Bund Deutscher Mädel (League of German Girls, a Nazi organisation). She asked the priest some questions: 'Was Jesus a Jew? Did the Jews kill him? Should the Jews be shunned?' but he could not or was not allowed to answer:

> My misgivings and distress increased. And the hate campaign, which began against the Jews, became noisier and clearer. Our landlord, Herr Frühling, for

example, was a dear man. Whenever he went shopping on a Saturday to the Altstadt market he came back with gifts for us of cherries, apricots or apples. He always had a friendly word. Why should we suddenly treat him differently? Why did the Nazis now revile him? We wouldn't have anything said against our dear Herr Frühling. The wicked rabble-rousers surely did not know him. If they did wouldn't they like him as much as we did?[13]

In 1938, in the weeks after *Kristallnacht*, many of the Jews in Königsberg were marched off to concentration camps for a few weeks as a warning that they were no longer welcome in the city; the aim was not to murder them but to encourage them to leave. Little is recorded about the experiences of the Königsberg Jews in these camps, but elsewhere in Germany it was well known that most of those arrested were bullied, starved, physically abused and in some places tortured. Eventually most of the prisoners began to drift back home, usually after hints that their departure from Germany would be welcomed. As a result about two-thirds of Königsberg's Jewish families (about 3,000 people) left before the outbreak of the Second World War, travelling by train across the Polish Corridor to Berlin and then on to Bremerhaven from where they could sail to Britain or the USA. Those who remained behind were forced into labour battalions and had to move into specially designated accommodation.

In July 1941 Hermann Göring ordered Reinhard Heydrich, head of the SS Security Service, to prepare 'a general plan of the administrative, material and financial measures necessary for carrying out the desired final solution to the Jewish question'. This plan was ultimately finalised at the Wannsee Conference on 20 January 1942 when the decision was taken to start on the programme of mass extermination, but before this, on 3 September 1941, the order came that all Jews over six years of age were to wear yellow stars on their coats and jackets. The stars were as large as the palm of the hand and were printed with a black letter 'J'. Now the Jews were marked for all to see and they were barred from participating in normal everyday life. Just over a month after the stars were ordered came the decree forbidding any further Jewish emigration from the Reich.

From that time on, Michael Wieck knew he could no longer believe he belonged in the city he loved:

> Up until then there were still moments when we could rent a boat and spend a carefree hour during nice weather on the castle pond . . . or take a train out to the suburbs to go swimming. Now it took quite a bit to gather up the courage to step out onto the street as a marked person. I had to walk in the gutter and it was shocking to be spat on . . . It seems to me that they succeeded in stirring up the population of East Prussia particularly well, probably the result of many diatribes by the ambitious and pathologically anti-Semitic Gauleiter, Erich Koch.[14]

In 1942 the final expulsions began; at first it was small groups of elderly Jews who received notices for 'resettlement', and then in June it was the turn of families in which no one worked in an essential job. They were mainly sent to camps at Riga and Minsk or to Theresienstadt. Dora Skopp's Uncle Walter had been drafted into the police. One of his tasks was to check the contents of trains arriving and leaving the Hauptbahnhof. One day he came to their house in a terrible state. He had been to the station and seen a train loaded not with goods, but with people. They were Jews being sent to labour camps in Russia. All around were members of the SS armed with machine guns and they were forcing the Jews onto the train. They shot anyone who tried to escape. When Dora told her school friends how shocked she was by this, her class teacher came to see her father and told him that she would be reported to the police if she ever said anything in defence of the Jews again.[15]

On the day Michael Wieck's Aunt Rebekka was 'resettled', over 1,000 Jewish people from Königsberg were put on to special trains. A few weeks later, in the Adas Israel synagogue, he became aware of the despair and hopelessness of the situation. 'There are an especially large number of empty places. Everyone has relatives, friends, acquaintances amongst those deported.' Nevertheless there was a little comfort. Klaus, his 'Hitler Youth neighbour' remained a good friend and there were others who 'slipped bread ration cards into our mailbox from time to time' and music-loving friends 'who frequently made declarations of sympathy to my parents'. Some Königsbergers, he realised, were aware of the terrible wrongs taking place and their own helplessness:

> But there were many without scruples who simply took advantage of everything those who were transported had abandoned: estates, houses, apartments, books and positions now vacant.[16]

Chapter Six

THE WAR

The Second World War began on 1 September 1939 when Hitler invaded Poland. Hitler believed the invasion was justified:

> Danzig was and is a German town. The Corridor was and is German. The whole area owes its culture to German civilisation. Danzig will be retaken by us. The Polish Corridor will be annexed.[1]

When the invasion was complete the newly appointed Gauleiter of Danzig, Albert Forster, issued a proclamation thanking God for the 'release':

> We, the people of Danzig, are overjoyed that now we are again citizens of the Reich. In these happy times we will stand together and give thanks to the Führer that he has brought us back into Greater Germany.[2]

Sybil Bannister was not surprised by the take-over for she had seen preparations being made for several months. A 4,000-strong army of ex-soldiers had been formed in Danzig in June 1939 and SA men had been preparing defences around the city at night. On 25 June a thousand SS men from East Prussia and a number of SS officers from Germany had arrived, ostensibly for a sporting contest with the local SS, but a considerable number did not leave after the competition was over.[3] More and more young men appeared in SS-style uniforms but with '*Heimwehr Danzig*' – 'Home Guard Danzig' – on their sleeves. In the same month former barracks were occupied and houses requisitioned for the storage of ammunition. Some 2,000 men were working twenty-four hours a day in shifts constructing barracks to accommodate 10,000 men.

In Königsberg a disused hotel, the Reichsgarten, was opened up and the downstairs areas were organised as lecture rooms. Local people were encouraged to come and learn about protection against air attacks and how to be an air-raid warden. There was also instruction in first aid. In rural East Prussia farmers were asked to give up over sixty per cent of their horses to the armed forces and young men were called up for six weeks of military exercises.

At the end of June the German government notified the Polish government that the warship *Königsberg* would visit Danzig for three days beginning on 25 August, although it was the *Schleswig Holstein* which eventually came. Sybil saw that, 'The Polish Government was of course aware that the gradual remilitarisation of the Free City of Danzig could prove dangerous to them, but they did not seem seriously alarmed.' Yet all the time she felt that she was 'walking on a volcano'. In August her 'nerves were shattered by reports of further trouble between the Polish and Danzig customs officials'.[4] For the first time the German government openly intervened in the dispute saying that, if the Poles continued to cause economic losses to Danzig, the city would have no other choice but to seek other opportunities of exporting and importing goods. In other words Germany would open the Danzig–East Prussia border.

Still the Poles did not seem unduly alarmed. They did not

consider it likely that Hitler would go to war – and they were taken aback when, on 23 August, the Non-Aggression Pact between Germany and the Soviet Union was announced. The pact secretly guaranteed that the Soviet Union would allow Germany to move into western Poland and the Polish Corridor whilst Stalin could have a free hand in eastern Poland, Finland and the Baltic States. Hitler issued the orders for the attack on Poland two days later and on Friday 1 September the citizens of Danzig were awoken by the sound of gunfire and at 5.00 a.m. the proclamation came that Danzig had been returned to the Reich and that German forces had entered Poland.

The truth of the matter was that, although the area that was 'liberated' by the German attack, Danzig, West Prussia, and the Wartheland, had 20 million inhabitants, 17 million of them were Poles and fewer than a million were German. Despite this the occupying Germans now began a process of evacuating many of the Poles and other groups such as the Jews. The plan was that supposedly ethnic Germans who lived elsewhere in eastern Europe, known as the *Volksdeutsch*, would be brought to live in West Prussia, which was now to be Germanised, as part of a policy called '*Heim ins Reich*'.

The division of Poland resulted in 21.5 million people being transferred to Germany and 13.5 million to the Soviet Union. The pact between the two countries also included an agreement on the movement of peoples from the respective spheres of influence. Germany decided to evacuate 60,000 Baltic Germans from Estonia and Latvia, as part of *Heim ins Reich*, to make a new home in the Fatherland (mostly in Poland). Ships were sent to the ports of Riga and Tallinn to pick them up. In August 1940, after the Baltic States had been incorporated into the Soviet Union, the German ambassador met his Russian counterpart in Riga and expressed his congratulations on the satisfactory completion of the annexation process. But, if Stalin was lulled into a false sense of security by these events, he was soon to find out the truth.

In a programme of ethnic cleansing, the SS massacred thousands of Poles and Jews, and at least a million were forced to move east to an area of Poland near Cracow, named by the Germans the 'General Government'. Hitler's orders were that in the General Government, 'They should be pushed into a reduced state and left entirely to themselves.' It would be run like a German colony, the standard of living would be kept deliberately low and it would be a source of slave labour when needed.

At night the Gestapo began to swoop down upon the Poles in their homes and turn them out into the street, without giving them a chance to take their belongings. Those Poles, mainly of mixed ethnicity, who were allowed to remain, were spurned and oppressed unless they agreed to become *Volksdeutsch*. This allowed them to have identity and ration cards in return for swearing loyalty to the Reich. Nevertheless, they were made to move out of the best houses and flats into dismal quarters, again always by night. Carts trundled through the dark streets loaded with women and children huddled on top of their hastily packed goods. They were forbidden to speak Polish and if they were overheard doing so on the street they were punished. Germans and Poles were segregated on every occasion, the Poles being given the remains after the Germans had taken their pickings. They could only work as labourers because no German would shop in a Polish store, nor go to a Polish doctor or dentist. As the Germans were the only people with money it very soon meant bankruptcy for Poles to try set up independently, even if they did get permission to do so – which was unlikely. All official positions were of course given to Germans.

There followed the first Nazi attempt at the wholesale resettlement of a people in the newly expanded Reich. In December 1939 police commandos began to clear houses to allow the *Volksdeutsch* to move in. Those thrown out were deported in goods wagons in freezing weather to the General Government. The people of Poland were never to forget the terrible treatment meted out to them by the Germans. At the same time, the Russians who had invaded eastern Poland also evacuated Poles, Jews and White Russians to Siberia and Central Asia.

By this time Germany was at war. British and French intervention after the invasion of Poland had taken Hitler by surprise. Their willingness to compromise over Czechoslovakia in 1938 had led him to believe that the invasion of western Poland would invite no reprisals. The British were not great supporters of the Danzig Corridor and believed that Germany had justifiable reasons for wanting Danzig back. Nevertheless, Hitler's contemptuous breaking of the terms of the Munich Agreement on Czechoslovakia forced the British government to reassess Hitler's ambitions in Poland. Soon after Hitler had come to power in 1933 the British commentator William Harbutt Dawson had warned:

> No one should ignore the effects of the treaty, which cuts Germany into two parts, and severs Danzig, one of the most German of cities, from the fatherland. Can Europe afford to ignore this menace and allow matters to drift? To do so would be tantamount to inviting and hastening catastrophe.[5]

On 2 September 1939, following the German attack on Poland, the British and French governments sent Hitler ultimata demanding the withdrawal of German troops by 11.00 the following morning. When Hitler failed to respond, they declared war on Germany.

The outbreak of war was not greeted with enthusiasm in Germany but in Königsberg, at least outwardly, everyone seemed to be for the war. Although there was no public rejoicing as there had been in 1914, there was also little anxiety. People recall that many had great faith in Hitler.[6] In Palmnicken, a few miles away on the Baltic coast, the local brass band turned out to play tunes with rousing titles such as 'People to Arms!' or 'In the East Do You See the Dawn?'[7] but in contrast von Papen prophesied disaster and in Berlin people watched the cavalcades of soldiers passively; there was little cheering, singing or waving of flags and the older people who remembered the First World War were pessimistic about the future.

Perhaps aware of the lack of enthusiasm for war, Hitler's intention was that the civilian population should be protected as much as possible from hardship. In order to ensure adequate supplies for all, for the duration of what was hoped would be a short war, ration cards were issued in the first few weeks after war broke out. Rationing was not an immediate necessity because Germany had spent the previous five years working to be self-sufficient and had amassed enormous reserves of food. However, the decision was made to begin rationing from the very start of the war to avoid the impact of having to reduce food availability at a later stage. The system was very complicated with different coloured sheets of paper for different products: yellow for butter and cheese, blue for meat, brown for bread, white for sugar, orange for clothes, and so on. The bread squares were mostly for rye bread and could be spent on pumpernickel, wholemeal rye bread or grey bread which was a more refined but less tasty version of rye bread. In Königsberg the shops still seemed to have plenty of provisions and, until rationing started, people went on a buying spree stocking up with coffee, tea, nuts, dried fruit and sugar. Each household was ordered to prepare sandbags and to line roofs with fireproof material,[8] and gas masks were distributed.

The most keenly felt immediate effect was the blackout which was imposed from the first day of the war. The blackout requirements were very demanding and Nazi officials made tours of inspection. In some places the only blackout material available was black paper which was difficult to manage and to keep in place.

The blackout made life very difficult, particularly for townsfolk. Agnes Marie Grisebach, who lived in the Baltic port of Rostock when the war broke out, remembers one autumn evening in 1939 when she was finding her way home in complete darkness. Suddenly the sky came alight with a display of lights which looked like flames – orange, yellow, green, red and blue – accompanied by a humming noise. It lasted for about five minutes and then everything was dark. An old fisherman told her that she had seen the Northern Lights, and told her that he had heard from his grandfather that the same rare sight had appeared in the skies a few days before Napoleon invaded Russia. 'They meant bad luck,' he said, to which she replied, 'Let's hope Hitler doesn't decide to do the same.'[9]

Although there were more people in uniform on the streets of Königsberg, in the first months of the war East Prussia seemed safe and children from western parts of Germany were evacuated there. The ease with which Poland was conquered and the period of the Phoney War which followed resulted in a brief lull in tension. Friedrich von der Groeben remembers men coming back to his father's estate in East Prussia in the autumn to get in the harvest where they worked alongside Polish prisoners, and some of the family's horses were also returned.[10] For many months day-to-day life continued as it had always done. The University remained open and each Sunday people flocked to the Cathedral in all its splendour to pray for Germany. On warm evenings families strolled around the historic riverside warehouse district, the Speicher, enjoying the evening sun by the river and then eating and drinking in its many bars and restaurants. Fish was always in plentiful supply and the fishwives still came to the dockside markets to sell their catch. Although the regular military band concerts in the Castle courtyard came to an end when the war broke out, much of the city's cultural and musical life continued. The boys' choir, which was nationally famous, continued to give concerts until 1942. The city zoo remained open and attracted large numbers of visitors.

Economic confidence grew in the city as Königsberg benefited from the huge rise in demand for naval vessels and U-boats; the dockyards took on many hundreds of extra workers including slave labour from the conquered lands. At the peak of armaments production over 19,000 people were employed in these industries. The people of the province were also delighted that the Polish Corridor had been retaken. Sarah Collins, the English wife of a German doctor, travelling with her husband for a brief holiday through the old Corridor in 1940, noted how:

> People in the railway carriage drew our attention to what had been frontier stations. One old farmer from Tilsit said to me, 'You British people have one sensible man and that is Lloyd George. He knew how wrong it was to cut a Polish Corridor through German territory and separate East Prussia from the Fatherland.'[11]

Every school in Germany was required to have a big map of Europe on display and small flags were moved when news came of how far the German troops had advanced. In 1940 the maps of eastern Europe were put away and replaced by ones of France, Holland and Belgium. As each conquest was announced on the radio every household had to hang out at least one swastika flag to celebrate another victory, and indeed the ease with which Western Europe was conquered at small military cost engendered a feeling of euphoria. Military successes were broadcast over the radio each night and schoolchildren all over Germany had to listen to repeat broadcasts in the afternoon when the announcements were made slowly, three words at a time, and each child had to write them down laboriously.

Major victories, such as the fall of Paris, were given special status. The announcer interrupted programmes every five minutes to say that a special communiqué was coming until the announcement was due. Then there was a moment of silence during which restaurants and cafés were required by law to turn up the volume on their sets so that people on the streets could also hear the announcement, which was heralded by trumpets and then the playing of '*Die Wacht am Rhein*'. As the portentous words 'From the Führer's Headquarters' began, waiters were supposed to stop serving and the customers to fall silent. The easy victories on the Western Front had no direct effect on the people of East Prussia but, as country after country fell, belief in Hitler's invincibility grew apace. When Paris fell, Königsberg, like all other towns in Germany, flew Nazi flags and the church bells rang to announce such a famous victory. By the summer of 1940 the German Army controlled most of Western Europe; Britain stood alone against the Third Reich and Hitler believed it would not be long before this last enemy surrendered.

The people of Königsberg crowded into the cinemas to watch the newsreels of Hitler's triumphant return to Berlin on 6 July 1940; they saw the tens of thousands of Berliners lining the streets from the station to the Reich Chancellery and throwing flowers as Hitler passed by. Time and time again the Führer appeared on the balcony before the yelling throng and all Germany joined in a jubilant national celebration of the country's war success. The American journalist Howard K. Smith noticed the change in Hitler's demeanour 'now he was the greatest conqueror in the world, the most hated and the most loved man alive'. Smith saw the Führer chatting to Göring on the balcony that day while the crowds cheered. He saw how his walk had become 'graceful and confident' and his smile was firm with no sign of any remaining timidity. 'From the distance of ten feet, his eyes appeared no longer the eyes of a funny little man, but were calm, hard and cruel, like the apotheosis of the military man he had become.'[12] Berlin shone in his reflected glory; the cafés and restaurants were full, concert halls and theatres continued to see full houses, and booty from France, Belgium, and Holland poured in – silks, furs, perfumes and other luxury items.

Königsberg lay 600 kilometres east of Berlin and enjoyed none of this bounty. Even so morale in the town was high and there were few obvious hardships. Königsberg households benefited from the arrival of Poles who had been brought in as slave labour to work in factories or go into families as domestic help. Helga Gerhardi's mother, like most middle-class women, had had a live-in maid before the war but after that German girls were forbidden to go into domestic service and her mother had found it hard to manage their big house on her own. Most Germans at this time had a fairly low opinion of the Poles so it is not altogether surprising that Frau Gerhardi thought the first two Poles were 'hopeless girls'. They seemed to come from very primitive backgrounds and were frightened of all the new and modern equipment they found in a prosperous German bourgeois home. Both of them were unwashed, with matted hair, when they arrived and one of them had never seen a lavatory before. Helga had to demonstrate to her how it was used but when she pulled the chain 'she ran screaming to the locked front door' and tried to run away. Eventually a satisfactory maid, Olga, was obtained by bribing the manageress of the labour exchange with butter, cheese and coffee beans. Helga felt sorry for Olga, who was not supposed to leave her place of employment. She decided that, as Olga's German was quite good, for a Christmas treat she would take her to the cinema in central Königsberg. Having wrapped Olga up in one of Helga's old coats, they left the house separately and went to two different tram stops before taking the tram into the town centre:

> All went well, even at the cinema. Olga never said a
> word, as instructed, and would only reply with a yes or
> no to anything I asked her. After that we often went
> together, and she was most grateful, as she knew what
> a risk I took.[13]

Bombing raids on East Prussia were considered most unlikely but nevertheless precautions were taken in the towns. The authorities advised families to prepare cellars as possible bomb shelters and grants were made available to help pay for the alterations. There were air-raid practices and civilian firefighters were appointed and were required to undergo intensive training. In the summer of 1940 school-children were sent out into the woods to pick medicinal herbs; in the autumn they gathered acorns and horse chestnuts. In September they were expected to help with the harvest. In Königsberg most school children were required to do this *Erntedienst* – 'harvest duty' – and the autumn school term was made shorter because labour was needed on the farms to replace men who had joined the armed forces. Children and young women were sent from the city to live with farmers for a few weeks, and although school resumed when they returned there was still work to do. Nazi officials decreed that nothing should be wasted. Everything possible must be recycled and school children were needed to make house-to-house calls to advertise the collection and then take things to their school where everything was sorted and weighed. Amongst the changes *Eintopf*, a 'one-pot' meal, compulsorily replaced the traditional family Sunday lunch and the nominal saving of 50 pfennig had to be donated by each family to the Winter Programme. At Christmas that year children were asked to pack small parcels with gifts and send them with a letter to an unknown soldier at the front.

Despite such tasks, with Hitler's power at its height in 1940, spirits were generally high in Germany. People were well dressed and the cafés and theatres were busy, even though the Königsberg dance halls were closed. The Alhambra, one of the town's main cinemas, was always crowded with people eager to see one of the many cheery musicals and light comedies churned out by the Party to keep morale high (these films became more and more escapist as the war situation worsened). In these early months of the war the *Wochenschau*, the newsreels, which always preceded the main film at the cinema, were the way of informing audiences about the successes of the German armed forces. At first they were full of optimism and, along with the Nazi press, these newsreels declared it was impossible for Germany to lose the war. Even at Christmas 1940, when news came from the west of the first significant British air raids on German cities, most people remained confident that the war would soon be over.

Although families in Königsberg were not exempt from their menfolk being called up to fight in the war, the first serious impact on the general population did not occur until the early spring of 1941. Troops, tanks and equipment, much of it arriving by sea at Pillau, came through East Prussia and moved into occupied Poland by road or rail. The whole area became a great army camp and yet the general view in Königsberg was that the troops were getting ready for spring training in April. The Nazi authorities told local people that the men were indeed simply on manoeuvres but by June it had became clear that they were part of something bigger – the force which eventually invaded Russia on 22 June 1941.

The radio announced the invasion that evening and between the bulletins military marches were played. Hitler issued a proclamation to the German nation saying that although 'his heart had bled within him' he had had to act before the Soviet Army struck at Germany. The next night Russian planes flew over Königsberg and bombs fell near the gas works and in the suburbs. There were no further attacks, for the Luftwaffe successfully wiped out most of the Russian air fleets almost immediately afterwards; tranquillity returned to the city.

With food supplies well managed, the Germans had eaten reasonably well for the first twenty-odd months of the war, but after the launch of the Russian campaign the situation deteriorated rapidly in most of the Reich. Both the quality and the quantity of the rations declined swiftly. Within five months of the launch of Operation Barbarossa the meat ration of 500 grams per week had been reduced to 160. Vegetables became luxuries and other necessities of life such as soap and toothpaste became scarcer. The quality of the food available grew poorer and it became impossible to buy new clothes or shoes. As hardship increased the general health of the population declined and a severe shortage of tobacco forced the Nazi authorities to give the Hitler Youth lectures on the harm that smoking could do to their health. A new rule was introduced which forbade the selling of cigarettes to women.

The food shortages were compounded by the need to recruit more and more men into the armed forces to serve on the Russian Front, leaving farms devoid of labour. Christmas 1941 was gloomy The shops were empty, except, as Howard K. Smith saw in Berlin, 'the toy shops where there were lots of cardboard games, like one called "Bombs on England". There was no liquor for Christmas punch, and there were no geese or rabbits for Christmas dinner.' He noticed how pale the people had become 'unhealthily white as flour, except for red rings around their tired lifeless eyes.'[14]

Even in well-provided-for Königsberg, it was impossible to ignore the number of wounded soldiers who passed through the city on their way back to military hospitals in the west and a great war weariness set in as civilians struggled to cope with filling the gaps on the farms and in the factories. The problem was partially solved by the Nazi authorities providing slave labourers from the countries they had conquered. In East Prussia most of these were Poles and Ukrainians, many of whom came from very poor rural areas. They were rounded up by the SS and brought to East Prussia. Polish workers had to wear a P on their clothes and the Russians the word 'Ost'. They were given food and shelter in return for working on the farms but the regulations stated that there was to be no social contact between them and the Germans. In Königsberg industrial and military production was also maintained in part by workers who were regarded as inferior: prostitutes, deported Russian girls, French prisoners of war, Poles, gypsies and the few remaining Jews.

Marianne Mackinnon, sent from Berlin into the Prussian countryside to work in 1942, found herself in a family which was most enlightened. At supper on her first evening, which in typical Prussian fashion consisted of a steaming meat stew, dripping thick with onions and apples, and thick slices of bread, she was introduced, by Herr Hansen, the farmer, to Janislav, a Pole:

'You might as well know', he said, that 'when they brought him here they left instructions on how he was to be treated. Jan is not allowed to go to the next village, not even to church. He is not supposed to listen to the radio or read a newspaper. He must not sleep under the same roof as us and should take his meals in the shed where he lives. They told us not to get too chummy with him; there are hefty penalties for that sort of thing. But I say "bull shit". He's more like a member of the family; out here a man is as good as his work and I will not have a man treated like an animal on my property. Mind you, when Herr Stiller is here – he's the rural inspector, *Parteigenosse* [Party stalwart], a real Hitler fanatic they say; you know "Heil Hitler" here, "Heil Hitler" there – I shout a bit at Jan to make Herr Stiller think I'm keeping Jan on a tight rein!'

Herr Stiller, she continues, was:

... a pompous, rotund Party official and regional agriculture inspector, appointed to spot check on home slaughter and to ensure the timely delivery of fixed quotas. Herr Hansen called him a *Schmeissfliege* [bluebottle] for buzzing round like a tiresome insect, for Herr Stiller liked to boost his own rations and was in the market for favours and counter-favours. One day, slapping the dough she was kneading, as if it were Herr Stiller's pot-belly, Frau Hansen summed up her contempt for this reputed model of political perfection: 'That man would sell his daughter for a pound of butter and a dozen eggs!'[15]

The New Year, 1942, began with orders from Hitler that the home front should produce a maximum effort. Even more recruits were needed for the armed forces and those left at home should do everything they could to increase production. Most of the effort was concentrated on munitions and as a result consumer goods disappeared from the shops. Food supplies dwindled even more rapidly in 1942 and rations were sharply reduced. By the end of 1942 there was no milk available for adults in most of Germany, potatoes were rationed and vegetables were in short supply. Their main drink was tea made from dried blackberry leaves, strawberry leaves, mint and tree bark chopped very small. Christmas 1942 was miserable in much of Germany, although in East Prussia food continued to be produced in relative abundance and prudent housewives preserved and bottled as they had always done. Farmers were the best off since they always kept plenty of their produce for their own consumption. They could also barter for goods that were otherwise unobtainable. For example a piece of fat bacon could be swapped for leather which would then be made into shoes in return for butter.

Marianne Mackinnon was only one of thousands of young women sent to work on the farms of East Prussia. She compared the frugal fare at home with the food available on the farms, where people gorged themselves:

> ... on thick meat stews, potato pancakes and soups enriched with hefty chunks of smoked pork. The sausages were home-made, the bacon farm-smoked; milk came in jugs straight from the cows, butter from the churn. At weekends there was *Topfenkuchen*, a cake rich in butter and eggs, whilst in baskets all over the house the first fruit was waiting for the bite of teeth.[16]

Holiday-makers were not allowed to share the relative plenty of the Königsberg district. The previous summer Sarah Collins had visited the Baltic coast near Königsberg.

She watched hungry holiday-makers, often escaping temporarily from the bombs in their home towns, who spent their days wandering around hoping to get a *Stammessen* – a couponless meal – to supplement the meagre fare on offer at the hotels and boarding houses.

Sarah Collins recalls that, after a miserable Berlin Christmas, she and her family were cheered by a visit from East Prussia:

> Herbert Wachtel came to visit us bringing with him a dozen eggs and rashers of home-cured bacon, which he had from his uncle's farm in East Prussia. He told me that he had brought all these good things for supper, and insisted that I cooked the whole dozen eggs, which seemed to me at that time to be a deed almost sacrilegious. We retired to the kitchen; I took the largest frying pan I had for the rashers of bacon, and into the large pan in which I had roasted the goose for Christmas before the war, I broke the twelve eggs, and all three of us watched fascinated as the whites gradually became opaque. I made tea from my iron reserve and just when I took the slice to lift the eggs out of the pan the air-raid siren sounded its melancholy warning and immediately everything was in tumult.[17]

Nevertheless, in Königsberg the cafés served imitation coffee and the cakes came not with the traditional piles of *Schlagsahne* (whipped cream) but with a flour-based substitute. The most fashionable café, Schwermers, with its terrace looking over the Schlossteich, no longer sold alcohol and by 1941 its famous marzipan was almost impossible to get hold of. At this time the Königsberg SS were constantly on the look-out for people in the city who were suspected of hoarding food. Helga Gerhardi recalls how her mother tried to hide the fact that they had bottled meat in their cellars by sticking large labels on the jars to hide the contents:

> We called them plums 2, or cherries 2, or blueberries 2, the number meaning it was meat, and plums meant pork, cherries chicken and blueberries beef. We also mixed the jars up with the fruit and we pushed the smelly sauerkraut barrel to the front of the cellar. My mother said that if I was at home and the SS came I should get some sauerkraut out when they went into the cellar to make it smell really bad. This might make them leave the cellar quicker![18]

Königsberg was much more fortunate than elsewhere in Germany. There had been no serious bombing of the city, although underground bunkers had been prepared. Since there were not enough of them to provide shelter for the whole population, people who were entitled to go into them were issued with a special pass which would have to be shown before they would be allowed in. Those who did not have such passes were advised to strengthen their cellars in case of a bombing raid.

From the summer of 1942, Königsberg was used as a collecting and assembly point for the armed forces heading for the Eastern Front. The Hauptbahnhof was crowded with military personnel arriving in and leaving the city. Many of them were foreign – from Romania, Slovakia, Hungary and Italy – and most of them did not speak German The foreign troops were mainly billeted in the suburbs but on their days off they came into the city centre and their lively chatter, even on one occasion in Spanish, created, in this northern city, an exotic cosmopolitan atmosphere very different from anything experienced before. Airmen from the much expanded airfield at Neukuhren, formerly a popular resort, on the Baltic coast, also came into the city on their days off and joined the others troops who visited the Castle. They boated on or strolled by the Castle Lake, walked in the parks and crowded into the cafés to drink *ersatz* coffee (probably made from a mixture of parsnips, acorns and barley)[19] and cakes with imitation cream. They were a great attraction to local girls who came to know that different countries had different days off – there were Hungarian afternoons, Italian afternoons and so on.[20] Back at the coast the airmen spent their leisure hours going to the beach a few minutes' walk from the airfield where they swam and sunbathed. The girls from Königsberg were easily persuaded to come and join them using the Samland railway from the North Station to Neukuhren.

In these coastal resorts men who were too old to serve in the Army had been ordered to form a coastal watch. They wore a grey Army-style uniform but received their orders from the Navy.[21] One of their tasks was to patrol the shores to look for mines and unexploded torpedoes, and then to call in the experts to defuse them and make the beaches safe for civilians and the airmen to relax.

Now there were always wounded soldiers in the city and accommodation became short because the bigger houses in the town had been commandeered for the Army. Schools were turned into Red Cross hospitals for injured soldiers from the Russian Front and the SS surveyed houses and flats, telling people what they could have and what they had to give up.

In the winters of both 1941–2 and 1942–3 German troops on the Russian Front suffered so badly that public appeals were made for skis, fur coats, rugs, boots, woollen underwear and mitts. Goebbels instituted a nationwide campaign to collect warm clothing of all kinds to be sent to the soldiers on the Eastern Front. Every household was asked to give heavy shoes, woollens and furs – these would have to be sacrificed because the needs of the soldiers enduring the Russian winter were greater than those of the people at home. Skis also had to be sent to the Eastern Front and, to prevent people skiing for sport, it was made illegal to travel on trains with skis. The Nazi official in charge of each street, the *Blockleiter*, was sent to check that people gave generously. As a result of such diligence, throughout Germany half a million fur coats, one and a half million jerseys and thousands of pairs of skis and ski boots were collected. Few reached the soldiers because of poor planning and lack of transport and much that was collected piled up in warehouses before finally being burnt. By this stage in the war clothing was a great problem for German civilians too; clothing coupons were distributed but the shops were bare and the sacrifice of these warm garments was an enormous one to have to make.

Most of the resorts along the Kurisches Nehrung were full of soldiers on leave in East Prussia or passing through on their way to the Russian Front. They had many stories to recount of the Russians' fanatical zeal and their determination to win whatever the cost to themselves. The Red Army was poorly equipped and badly organised but its soldiers' hatred of the Germans was such that they were prepared to sacrifice everything to defend their country.

At this time Königsberg railway stations were choked with seething masses trying to get on and off the trains. Military personnel were always given priority, as were members of the Hitler Youth and lads going off to do labour service. In the summer of 1943 more and more wounded soldiers turned up in Königsberg along with sailors whose ships came into the harbour for refits; by the end of 1943 Königsberg was also filling up with evacuees from the bombed cities of western Germany. There were a great number of foreign workers and soldiers on leave from the Eastern Front and Russian prisoners of war were locked up in the Castle. The population of the city had never been so large and as a result food had to rationed much more severely as were both gas and electricity. Despite this, in East Prussia and Königsberg people had enough of most basic necessities and could still obtain extras on the black market from the surrounding countryside. Although there was no petrol for private cars, the city trams and trains continued to run, though less frequently than before the war. Tickets were sold only for short journeys except to people in uniform.

Christmas 1943 was peaceful. Most people were able to enjoy the traditional fare of roast goose and red cabbage. People who lived there recall that the Christmas trees even had candles, though they were mostly left over from the previous year. In contrast, in Berlin, the privation was severe. Bread rations were cut to four slices a day and there was a severe potato shortage. Bread was baked from a mixture of 45 per cent rye, 35 per cent wheat and 20 per cent barley. It was crumbly and unappetising.

The winter of 1943–4 was very cold. In East Prussia the temperature sometimes fell as low as –25 degrees Celsius and the freezing weather lasted many weeks. Newsreels showed pictures of soldiers on the Russian Front suffering in temperatures as low as –40. The hospitals in Königsberg received troops suffering with severe frostbite; their fingers and toes fell off because of the cold and many had to have limbs amputated because after the frostbite gangrene set in. More and more nurses were transferred to the Eastern Front yet the number of wounded men being brought back to Königsberg grew all the time. The military hospitals in Königsberg were used as transit hospitals. The doctors did amputations, removed bullets and shrapnel, pinned bones and put splints on arms and legs. The injured were then sent west for further treatment.

The news broadcast on the radio was that the German Army was planning a fresh offensive against the Russians in the New Year, but those who nursed the wounded in Königsberg hospitals heard accounts of setbacks on the Eastern Front which contradicted the official version of events. By the beginning of 1944 it was clear to most civilians in East Prussia that the war would sooner or later be lost. Air raids on German cities were relentless, rations were cut further, and newsreels showed pictures of the results of the heavy bombing. Those with relatives in the west heard gruesome stories of people killed, buried under rubble, suffocated, incinerated, widowed and orphaned. New regulations were issued that all seventeen-year-olds were to leave school and do war work – the boys to the Army and the girls to whatever tasks were needed. As the weeks went by people became more and more anxious; would the time come when they would have to choose between leaving their homes and staying on waiting for what the newspapers called 'the bloody terror of the Bolshevist beasts'?

A view across the River Pregel to the Kneiphof Island and Cathedral in the 1920s.
(Bildarchiv Marburg)

The Schlossteich Brücke, the footbridge across the Castle Lake (Schlossteich)
leading to Königsberg Castle. The Castle's towers had dominated the city
landscape since the Middle Ages.

A peaceful scene of the Castle Lake and Castle.

The bustling Kaiser Wilhelm Platz at the foot of the main entrance to Königsberg Castle. This was one of the busiest traffic intersections in the city.

The Ostmesse; built in the 1920s as a trade fair centre it later became the location for Nazi Party rallies.

Smaller ships continued to enter the old Königsberg harbour in the town centre until the end of World War II.

The main building of the Albertina University, erected between 1846 and 1867.

The inner harbour where small ships unloaded their cargoes on to the town centre quays. *(Bildarchiv Marburg)*

View across the Hönig Brücke to the New Synagogue in the Lindenstrasse. The building was completed in the late nineteenth century for Königsberg's growing Jewish population.

The Stock Exchange situated by the Grüne Brücke across the River Pregel.

Above: The Krämer Brücke in the aftermath of one of the British air raids of 1944. Königsbergers begin to go about their business, trying to ignore the burnt corpse lying by the side of the road.

Right: A group of Soviet JSU-152 heavy self-propelled guns moves into position in a pine wood outside Königsberg, ready to take part in the bombardment of the city, March 1945.

A Soviet military policeman directs vehicles from Third Belorussian Front entering East Prussia ('Vostochnaya Prussiya' on the sign) at the start of the Soviet offensive to capture the province, January 1945.

T-34/85 tanks carry Soviet infantry into position for the assault on Königsberg, Third Belorussian Front, April 1945.

Above: A wrecked German gun position on the outskirts of Königsberg, smashed by the overwhelming Soviet bombardment.

Top left: Heavily laden Soviet trucks drive past a destroyed Jagdpanzer IV assault gun during the advance through East Prussia, March 1945.

Above: Attacking Russian infantry move along the banks of the sea canal in Königsberg during the final capture of the city, 6–9 April 1945

Left: Il-2 Shturmovik ground-attack aircraft flying low over the East Prussian countryside on their way to attack Königsberg, 6 April 1945.

Left: 'Für Uns' – 'For Us' – a German memorial to the dead of the First World War stands amid the destruction of Königsberg, April 1945.

Bottom right: Soviet tanks and assault guns in Kaiser Wilhelm Platz in front of the ruins of Königsberg Castle after the occupation of the city, as seen on the cover of a contemporary Soviet magazine.

Below: A German Königstiger heavy tank abandoned on the beach of the Frisches Haff, April 1945.

Above: Wrecked German vehicles and equipment litter the shore of the Frisches Haff after the final German defeat.

Left: Abandoned and wrecked German equipment in the Samland area of East Prussia, the last part of the region to hold out against the Soviet attacks, May 1945.

Below: A Jagdpanzer IV assault gun (*left*) and other smashed armoured vehicles line the sides of a Königsberg street shortly after the surrender.

German prisoners in Königsberg, April 1945. Clearly some of those captured are only boys, presumably former Hitler Youth now serving in the Volkssturm

Soviet troops on the attack against the Samland pocket, the last German-held part of East Prussia, mid-April 1945.

Debris litters the street and the ruined skeleton of the Castle looms ahead,
Königsberg, April 1945.

Königsberg civilians pick their way through the wreckage of their city, Münzstrasse,
April 1945.

Königsberg Cathedral, wrecked in 1944–45 and left in ruins, is now being restored with the help of contributions from Germany.

A few parts of the old city were not destroyed in the 1945 fighting and remain visible today. This is the Königstor, one of the old city gates.

Chapter Seven

As You Sow . . .

'Do you know Berlin?' asked Howard K. Smith in the last few weeks of 1941:

If you do, maybe you'd like to know what that grand old city looks like now that it has become the capital of all Europe.

The whole Nazi contrivance seemed to have been precisely so constructed that it would run along nicely without a single complaint until one fine day the whole thing, and all its parts, would go to pot at once; the axle would break, the tongue and the bridle, and every spoke decay all at once. Berlin is now a crippled shadow of its former self. All the little things that make life pleasant have disappeared. The shops are empty, shelves stone-bare. There is nothing except a lone worried salesman, who is always sorry. The changes began with the start of the Russian Campaign.[1]

On the night of 21 June 1941, more than 3 million German soldiers, 600,000 vehicles, 2,770 aircraft, 3,350 tanks and 650,000 horses massed along a 3,000-kilometre front stretching from the Baltic to the Black Sea. Their sights were trained on Russia. This force was to take part in Operation Barbarossa, one of the greatest campaigns in military history. The advance would be made by three army groups: Army Group North which aimed to secure Leningrad and the Baltic; Army Group South which would take Kiev and the coal- and oil-rich lands of the Ukraine and Caucasus; and Army Group Centre which would drive towards Moscow.

In the summer of 1940 Hitler had summoned Army leaders to draw up plans for an attack on Russia. The military chiefs believed that, in order to win, the German Army must aim to defeat the Russian armies near Russia's western borders. It would be dangerous if the Germans should allow themselves to be drawn far into the Soviet Union; if the Russians chose to fall back there was very little chance of achieving a final victory. The German generals were convinced, rightly as it turned out, that the Reich did not have the resources to cope with a long drawn-out war in the Soviet Union.

Hitler disagreed; the success of Germany's war effort in the west was so great that he could afford to brush aside the opinions of generals. He believed that the German Army could advance much farther east if they could create 'cauldrons' of intensive fighting in key locations – Leningrad, Moscow and Kiev – which would respectively open the doors to north, central and south-east Russia. Of these, Leningrad and Kiev would be the main targets, even though Moscow was the seat of government and the centre of transport, commerce and business. Many military leaders were appalled; 'When my staff spread out a map of Russia before me I could scarcely believe my eyes' said General Heinz Guderian.

The assault on Russia was the culmination of a long-standing obsession. Hitler had always wanted Russia's industries and agricultural lands as part of his *Lebensraum* or 'living space' for Germany and his Thousand-Year Reich. Russia had been on Hitler's agenda since he had written in *Mein Kampf* seventeen years earlier:

> We terminate the endless German drive to the south and the west of Europe, and direct our gaze towards the lands in the east. If we talk about new soil and territory in Europe today, we can think primarily only of Russia and its vassal border states.[2]

In expressing such opinions he was in tune not only with traditional German beliefs about the east but also with many contemporary German right-wing historians. One of these, Albert Brackmann, erstwhile professor at the Albertina University in Königsberg, believed that, 'The German people were the only bearers of civilisation in the East, and as the main power in Europe defended Western civilisation and brought it to the uncivilised nations.'[3] In a similar vein Otto Reche, who worked with Brackmann, recommended that:

> The German people must secure in Europe – and certainly now after the crushing of Poland – a large contained settlement area adequate for the greater German nation in the future . . . the German people need a new settlement area bordering their existing frontiers of at least 200,000 square kilometres.[4]

Since the 1930s, the Nazis had made the struggle against Bolshevism a central theme in domestic and foreign policy, and a war against Bolshevik Russia was the logical outcome of this belief. Hitler wanted to exterminate and enslave the 'degenerate' Slavs, whom he blamed for Communism, and he wanted to eradicate their 'Jewish Bolshevist' government before it could turn on him.

The 1939 pact with Stalin was only ever intended to give Germany time to prepare for war. As soon as Hitler had gained control of France, he looked east. Insisting that Britain was as good as defeated, he abandoned plans to invade and decided to finish off the Soviet Union as soon as possible, before it could significantly arm itself. 'We only have to kick in the front door and the whole rotten edifice will come tumbling down,' he told his officers.[5]

Superficially, his reasoning was sound, for Stalin had purged the Russian Army leadership in the late 1930s and the replacements, hastily promoted, lacked experience. Although some German Army chiefs had doubts about the wisdom of Hitler's decision to launch an attack on Russia they could not sidestep the fact that the German Army's *Blitzkrieg* tactics had had great success in Western Europe in 1940. It was hard to argue with Hitler's belief that the USSR would be 'one more lightning victory, particularly fought against the inferior races of the East'. It would establish the foundations of the Thousand-Year Reich by the annexation of the territory between the Vistula and the Urals and provide the source of much-needed raw materials, particularly oil.

Hitler was in no doubt that the German Army possessed better training, more extensive experience, and would have superiority at the points selected for attack. German intelligence had reported that the Russians were incapable of an offensive war because a large amount of their equipment was obsolete and poorly deployed, and also that they lacked good defensive positions. Hitler brushed aside warnings about the size and the inclement climate of the Soviet Union. Supremely over-confident, he believed that the German Army would defeat the USSR in two or three months, thought it unnecessary to prepare for a winter campaign, and failed to foresee the tenacity and dogged courage of the Russian people.

General Friedrich Paulus, then a senior staff officer, warned that a war against Russia would be unlike anything the Wehrmacht had ever tackled. The German armed forces were used to operating along comparatively small fronts but in the Soviet Union they would have to cover enormous distances and fan out to cover a 3,000-kilometre front. Even with 3 million men under arms they would be severely overstretched. Indeed, when the German Army rolled into Russia under the impression that there were 200 Russian divisions in total, it was to discover in the following months that there were over 400. The Germans knew that the Russian roads were poor and that the Russian railway tracks were of a different gauge to their own, yet these factors were not properly taken into account before the invasion took place. They were taken by surprise by the sheer vastness of Russia, the impassable mud tracks, the swamps, the forests and the endless steppes.

James Lucas, in his book *War on the Eastern Front*, captures well the feelings of the German soldiers as they faced the march across Russia:

> They were unprepared for the fields of sunflowers which went on for kilometre after kilometre after weary kilometre; solid blocks of colour stretching forward to the distant horizons. There were maize fields of unimaginable size and immense forests which were like jungles in the density of their tangled undergrowth. The German soldiers were unprepared for marshes so great in extent as to be as large as two provinces of their German homeland. They discovered that most roads were turned into impassable mud tracks following only moderate rainfall; that surfaces became deeply rutted through the weight of the traffic; that they were completely impassable in winter and in summer became dust traps.[6]

However, such experiences also reinforced the idea that Russians were lazy and incompetent. The Nazis believed that the Russians, like the Jews, merited contemptuous treatment, because of their racial inferiority. They were *Untermenschen* (sub-humans of lesser value). Prior to the invasion of June 1941, Hitler instructed the Army leadership to issue the so-called 'Commissar Order' which, among other things, provided for the execution of civilians. The soldiers of the German Army were to co-operate with special SS task forces – *Einsatzgruppen* – in rounding up Jews and Communist officials. They were so successfully indoctrinated against the Russians that few had any conscience about the way in which they were ordered to treat Russians, civilians and soldiers alike. It was put baldly in 1943 by SS chief Heinrich Himmler:

> What happens to a Russian, to a Czech, does not interest me in the slightest. Whether nations live in prosperity or starve to death interests me only so far as we need them as slaves for our culture; otherwise it is of no interest to me. Whether 10,000 Russian females fall down from exhaustion while digging an anti-tank ditch interests me only in so far as the tank ditch for Germany is finished.[7]

It was to be a racial and ideological war of the greatest savagery.

The early success of the Wehrmacht reinforced the concept of the inferiority of the Russians and other nationalities in the Soviet Union. German forces made spectacular gains in the first few weeks of the war. In the first two days half the Russian Air Force was wiped out, mostly while its aircraft were still on the ground, and Soviet armies were encircled with rapid pincer movements. It is estimated that, by mid-October 1941, the German Army had captured over 2 million Soviet soldiers. Many of those who surrendered expected treatment in line with the Geneva Convention, but of this the Germans took no notice. Many Russian prisoners of war were starved to death, and for the survivors conditions in their camps were dreadful. Little shelter was provided and rations were less than 1,000 calories a day. Prisoners who were too ill to work were shot. Others died because the German Army was ordered not to provide medical assistance to Russian prisoners of war; the Russians were only permitted to use Russian doctors, and Russian supplies, equipment, transport, and other facilities. As if this were not enough, the ill-equipped German soldiers began stealing winter clothes and boots from prisoners of war. Göring attempted to justify the treatment of Russian prisoners of war by claiming that the USSR had not signed the Geneva Convention.

The treatment of prisoners of war by the Wehrmacht was ruthless but it was not as bad as the treatment of civilians, who for the most part had not even fought the Germans, and in some cases were prepared to aid them. People of the Baltic States and the Ukraine initially saw the Wehrmacht as an army which had come to liberate them from Russian control, but Nazi propaganda had convinced the German soldier that he should view all Slavs as a 'conglomeration of animals'. Godfrey Lias, describing the experiences of the German Fourth Army in the Russian campaign, records how:

> Almost everywhere, when the German troops arrived, the inhabitants had welcomed them as liberators. We had seen them doing it and were sure they were sincere. We could both speak Ukrainian as well as Russian and we knew how the Ukrainian peasants hated the Bolsheviks, particularly Stalin, whom they regarded as responsible for changing Lenin's policy

and forcing them into collective farms, bringing famine and death to millions in the process. Both my friend Toni and I had talked to hundreds of prisoners and watched the eagerness with which they begged to be allowed to join a Liberation Army to fight their oppressors. The civilian population had greeted us both as friends. And then both of us noticed the change after the Ukraine had been made a German colony with Rosenberg [in charge], instead of being declared an independent colony.[8]

As in Poland, schools and universities in the Ukraine were shut down and hundreds of thousands were drafted into involuntary servitude in Germany. Between 1941 and 1944 2.5 million Soviet citizens, including hundreds of thousands of Ukrainians, were transported into Germany to work in industry and agriculture. Those left behind suffered the German Army looting their food, animals and carts as well as other possessions.

The Germans under their Nazi leaders were bent upon the enslavement of all *Untermenschen*. They were not interested in providing refuge or assistance to those who were anti-Soviet and were fleeing the Russians. In late July 1941, the German Army began to shoot all refugees. Civilians were also shot for reasons such as breaking curfew or being caught outside without a pass. In an effort to hamper partisan activity, houses in, which the Germans thought partisans were hiding were burned with the occupants inside. When winter came, the peasants were at the mercy of German soldiers. Many peasants were marched into woods or fields when the temperature was as low as −20 Celsius, stripped of their clothes, and left to freeze to death. Collective punishments were also used against civilians. For instance, on 30 January 1942, after a German sledge had driven over some mines which had been placed on the outskirts of the village of Nov Ladomiry, the whole male population of the village was shot and the houses burned down as a 'collective measure'.

The siege of Leningrad, which lasted for 900 days from 8 September 1941 until January 1944, was one of the most appalling manifestations of Nazi treatment of Russian civilians. The capture and submission of Leningrad had been a particular fixation in Hitler's mind because it was the seat of Communism and the source of the Bolshevik Revolution of November 1917. The unspeakable treatment of its citizens would be avenged in 1944 and 1945 when the Soviet Army invaded East Prussia, razed the city of Königsberg to the ground, and left those who survived to starve.

The German Army reached Leningrad comparatively easily in 1941 but at the end of August found its way into the city barred. With Leningrad encircled, Hitler gave orders to starve the city into submission and to then wipe it off the face of the earth. Some 2.9 million civilians, including about 40,000 children, and various units of the Red Army were trapped. The city had been under fire for several weeks and food and fuel supplies were only sufficient for a couple of months. On 6 September the Luftwaffe dropped thousands of incendiary bombs on the Badayev warehouses, a two-hectare site of wooden buildings that held much of the city's remaining food supplies; the next morning the whole city was suffused with the smell of burning meat, flour, lard and sugar. After this disaster the people of Leningrad had only a few weeks' supply of food left and there was little hope of receiving any more. With the city under constant bombardment, the situation became unbearably grim. There was no heating, no water supply, no electricity and very little food. People began to eat whatever they could find: first their pets, then the rats, and then wallpaper and even the plaster from the walls. Eventually they even turned to eating sawdust. They huddled together at night for warmth. Official rations had been reduced to 125 grams of bread per day. Thousands of people died; the eventual death toll was at least 630,000, although some estimates put it as high as 850,000. Most of these died of starvation.[9]

On 8 November 1941, in a speech in Munich, Hitler declared 'Leningrad's hands are in the air. It will fall sooner or later. No one can free it. No one can break the ring. Leningrad is doomed to die of famine.'[10] German radio began broadcasting to Leningrad the stark message, 'Leningrad will be compelled to surrender without the blood of German soldiers being shed.'[11] But, despite the rising death rate, the citizens were not ready to give in. They were preparing to use Lake Ladoga, to the east of the city, as a means of escape and a means of obtaining supplies. To this end a road was under construction linking the city with the lake. Lake Ladoga froze in the last week of November. Now limited supplies could be brought in lorries across the ice, but they came painfully slowly and the quantities they brought were small.[12] The death rate continued to rise to over 6,000 a day, for the city was starving and freezing to death. Nikolai Markevich wrote in his diary on 24 January 1942:

> The city is dead. There is no electricity, no trams.
> Warm rooms are rare. No water. Almost the only form
> of transport is sleds, carrying corpses in plain coffins,
> covered with rags or half clothed. Daily six to eight
> thousand die. The city is dying as it has lived for the
> last half year – clenching its teeth.

He could have added that there was no radio either and that it was one of the coldest winters anyone could remember.

Eventually the routes across Lake Ladoga were made safe enough to allow several hundred thousand to be evacuated in trucks across the frozen lake under constant German bombardment, via what became known as 'the road of life'. In four months more than half a million emaciated people were driven in trucks across the ice road, whilst in the opposite direction came fuel, ammunition and food. Evacuation continued by boat throughout the summer and from then until January 1944 the 600,000 who remained in the city struggled to hold the German Army at bay. The 900-day siege of Leningrad was the longest and most terrible endured by any city in modern times.

German methods only served to intensify the Russian determination to win the war and stiffened their resistance. Stalin and his generals appealed to the deep instincts of patriotism and love of the Motherland which was ingrained in nearly every Russian and as a result turned the Russian struggle into the Great Patriotic War. Ultimately, the racist ideology promoted by Hitler and the Nazis against the Russians was to lead to the superhuman effort made by the Red Army. The result was the final Soviet victory and the inevitable obliteration of Königsberg and East Prussia.

Chapter Eight

UNDER-ESTIMATING THE COLOSSUS

Germany's eventual defeat on the Eastern Front was the result of many grave miscalculations. From the first Hitler dangerously under-estimated the full extent of the Russian operation he had undertaken and the length of time it would take to complete and this led to the failure to prepare adequate equipment and reinforcements. The sheer size of Russia led to punishing advances across hundreds of kilometres of difficult terrain and made it impossible to provide adequate back-up to the troops as the German armies moved farther and farther away. The ferocity of the Russian winters was seriously misjudged. Hitler compounded his errors by his refusal to listen to the advice of his generals. Perhaps the biggest mistake of all was that Hitler allowed his contempt for the Russians to cloud his judgement about their response to the invasion of their country.

Nevertheless, in the first few months of the Russian campaign, Hitler's insistence that victory would be easy seemed well-founded. Until the German invasion was launched, Stalin, against all the evidence presented to him, persisted in his refusal to believe that the Germans were about to attack, and as a result he did not allow the Russian armed forces to make proper preparations for war. Intelligence about Hitler's plans had been available in the USSR in the summer of 1940; in July the NKVD, the Soviet intelligence agency, reported to the Kremlin that the German General Staff had asked the German Transport Ministry to provide data on rail capabilities for the movement of troops from west to east. A few months later, in November 1940, the Russian military began to give Stalin serious warnings of the danger of invasion but he refused to accept what they had to say; Stalin also turned a deaf ear to information which reached Moscow on 29 December 1940 that Soviet intelligence agencies had obtained an outline of Operation Barbarossa. 'It was clear that the General Staff did not anticipate that war would begin in 1941', wrote Marshal Voronov, wartime head of Soviet artillery, 'Stalin still clung to the belief that Hitler's intentions were honourable. He stated forcefully that he believed in the Non-Aggression Pact with Germany and had full confidence in it; he refused to see the obvious danger that threatened.'[1]

Why Stalin thought like this is difficult to explain. Richard Overy, in his book *Russia's War*, suggests that Stalin may have based his calculations on rationality: 'He argued that to invade the Soviet Union with its vast army and over stretched frontier would require a numerical advantage of two to one for the attacker. This Hitler did not have.' But this view, Overy suggests, may also have been due to a failure of imagination: 'He does not seem to have been able to entertain the idea that Hitler could undertake an assault so breathtaking, so against the grain of good military sense.'[2]

As a result of all this Russia was militarily not at all well prepared for the German invasion. Stalin had purged many of the most experienced army leaders in the late 1930s and this resulted in an acute shortage of trained commanders. He was forced to order the promotion of junior officers to replace them, but most of these lacked suitable experience of fighting or of commanding men. There was a huge reserve of manpower available to the Russian armed forces but the lack of good leadership meant that troops were badly deployed. Much of their equipment was old-fashioned and the training of tank and air crews had been badly neglected for many years. 'In the early stages of the war,' writes Gottlob Bidermann, 'we were facing a massive, unwieldy force that had been stripped of professional leadership and had been politically cleansed.'[3]

On 6 June 1941 Stalin belatedly approved a plan for a shift of Soviet industry to war production to be completed by June 1942. Yet the following week, on 14 June 1941, he ordered Soviet national newspapers to announce that the recent movement of German troops 'to the eastern and north-eastern regions of Germany must be presumed to be in connection with motives independent of Soviet–German relations.' This was followed by a declaration: 'Rumours of the intention to break the 1939 Pact are completely without foundation.' This report appeared just eight days before Operation Barbarossa was launched when it must have been clear that the massive German forces which been massing on Russia's western frontiers for weeks could only be there for one reason.

Before the outbreak of war with Germany, most Soviet manufacturing capacity was located in the western part of the country, particularly around Leningrad and in the eastern Ukraine. In June 1941 the Politburo created a Council for Evacuation to relocate these factories, which was led by N. A. Voznesensky, head of Gosplan, the Soviet industrial planning agency. In 1942 the relocation policy reached its peak. It was a massive undertaking; whole factories were moved eastwards well behind the front line – to Siberia, the Urals and Kazakhstan. For example, 8,000 rail trucks had to be used to move just one metallurgy company to the Urals and then the whole plant had to be reassembled in the most inhospitable of terrain. Once such moves were completed, hundreds of thousands of workers had to be housed and set to work in freezing conditions with few tools to make armaments, aircraft and tanks.

Although it was to prove effective in the end, the relocation of over 1,500 plants, 1,360 of which produced armaments, caused enormous disruption to output and it was over a year before production levels were restored. The battles of 1941 and 1942 had to be fought with existing stocks of weapons and ammunition. There were some plants which obviously could not be moved, such as the coal mines of the Donbas area and hydro-electric dams. In order to prevent such places falling into German hands they had to be destroyed. As on the land, the bulk of the work was done by women and children as all able men were required to serve in the army. Everyone was required to contribute to the war effort and they did so at enormous personal cost. Criminals and those unfortunate political prisoners who had been incarcerated in the *gulag* punishment camps of Siberia backed up the labour effort.

In the first few weeks of fighting, Russian losses were huge and the Soviet armies fell back in disarray; the Russian Air Force was shattered. In the late summer of 1941 it seemed as if German victory was inevitable. The Baltic States had been invaded; Smolensk, 300 kilometres from Moscow had been captured; Leningrad was under siege; and in September Kiev and Kharkov were taken.

Hitler was triumphant; on 24 June, only two days after the launch of Barbarossa, he arrived at his new headquarters in East Prussia, the Wolf's Lair, the *Wolfsschanze*, near

Rastenburg on the Steinort estate. Set deep in the forest, many regarded it as a gloomy place, 'a blend of monastery and concentration camp' as one Nazi general put it. It was tightly defended against attack; a system of walls, barbed wire and mines protected the bunkers and even Hitler was later to find the atmosphere there depressing. Nevertheless, it was from here he directed operations on the Russian Front and intended to preside over the swift victory he had promised.

The German people seemed persuaded; a Swedish journalist, Arvid Fredborg, attended a press conference in Berlin a couple of weeks after the invasion and asked when 'the big journalistic trip to Moscow would take place?' He was told 'that we should know by the middle or end of July', and he saw how 'the authorities and the people were carried away with joy'.[4]

Yet, as the German Army forged ahead, the soldiers met Red Army units prepared to fight with fanatical zeal. General Franz Halder, Army Chief of Staff, wrote presciently in his diary on 11 August 1941:

> The whole situation makes it increasingly plain that
> we have under-estimated the Russian colossus which
> is prepared for war with utter ruthless determination;
> our troops, sprawled over an immense front line, are
> subjected to the enemy's incessant attacks.[5]

Halder was right. The Russians had no intention of giving in, whatever the scale of their losses, and the war on the Eastern Front was to go on much longer than Hitler had intended. By the late summer of 1941 the German Army had already begun to flounder. There were simply not enough German soldiers to cover the vast front and German units became dangerously separated as immense gaps opened up between them. The Russian high command exploited this, and set about trying to separate units by driving attacks between them. By the end of September the German Army had lost nearly half a million men and Army leaders privately advised Hitler that the eastern campaign would have to continue well into 1942. The Soviet Union had not collapsed as Hitler had so confidently predicted and the Army faced a hard winter hundreds of kilometres from home in hostile terrain.

In Königsberg school buildings were commandeered as temporary hospitals for wounded soldiers from the Eastern Front at the same time as local cinemas showed pictures of the triumphant German advance. At Helga Gerhardi's school, they:

> ... took the flags out of our map in our class where only the occupation forces were stationed, like in Norway, France, the Balkan countries and Crete, and tried to carry on with the flags where the actual fighting was going on, like the Mediterranean and Russia. Living in East Prussia, we were very interested in the Russian war as it was on our doorstep and we all hoped it would be finished before the winter.[6]

But things were not going as well as the Germans had been led to believe. More and more families received letters returned from the front marked 'Fallen' in red ink, and the quick victory which Hitler had promised had not materialised. In September 1941 Howard K. Smith noticed that, in contrast to their previous optimism, a 'moral depression' now set in amongst German civilians. The Army's failure to secure victory on the Eastern Front had caused a feeling of great pessimism: 'People were dangerously out of sorts and anti-Nazi slogans were being painted on fences and buildings.'[7]

Since the start of Operation Barbarossa Hitler had disappeared from the public eye. Goebbels now persuaded him that he must address the German people and Hitler therefore spoke to them from the Olympic stadium in Berlin on 4 October 1941. He announced that the 'Soviet Army is beaten . . . the Bolshevik dragon is slain' and that Germany was on the brink of winning 'the greatest battle in the history of the world'.[8] Neither Howard K. Smith, nor the Swedish journalist Arvid Fredborg, was convinced. 'The performance', wrote Fredborg, 'was a display of Nazi stage-management. Hitler appeared forced, like a man playing his most important card and trying to persuade himself and others that it must go well.'[9] In marked contrast Bernt Engelmann, a boy from Hamburg who was twelve when Hitler came to power, recalls how his aunt and uncle, who were in the stadium along with thousands of other civilians, were utterly persuaded by Hitler's words. 'He's so wonderful' his aunt said of the Führer, 'There's no one like him in the whole world!' and her husband said, 'He convinced us completely. The Russians will be routed before the winter, and then the war will be over, thank God.' Together they pointed out the places in the Soviet Union which had already been conquered. 'The rest will collapse,' they reassured their nephew, 'It'll all be over in a week at most.'[10]

On 10 October a press conference was called at the Propaganda Ministry in Berlin. Hitler's chief press officer, Otto Dietrich, declared that that the last remnants of the Red Army were 'trapped in two steel vices which were tightening daily'. Moscow would soon undergo 'swift merciless annihilation' and between Germany and the complete conquest of the untold riches of Russia there remained only 'the time it takes man and machine to cover the given distance'. 'The Eastern Continent', Dietrich continued, 'lay like a limp virgin in the mighty arms of the lustful German Mars.'[11]

The German people were briefly taken in. The official newspaper, the *Völkischer Beobachter*, carried headlines the next day: 'The Great Hour Has Struck! Campaign in the East Decided'.[12] In Berlin civilians optimistically hung wreaths of roses on German tanks whilst bookshops began to stock sets of Russian grammars, but Arvid Fredborg was cynical: 'The feeling among the Scandinavians grew decidedly sceptical; there were so many circumstances that could not be explained.'[13] On 11 October 1941, the headline in the *Völkischer Beobachter* read 'Eastern Breakthrough Deepens'. On 12 October Germans read, 'Annihilation of Soviet Army Almost Concluded' and on 14 October, 'Operations in the East Proceed According to Plan'. A day later they simply read 'Operations in the East Proceed as Foreseen'.[14] It was clear to many that the rapid conquest of Russia was not going to be achieved.

Howard Smith recalls that, as early as mid-October, there was no longer any mention of the final victory though the newspapers continued to reassure readers that Moscow would be encircled and that Bolshevism and the Red Army would be finished off. By the end of October it became obvious that there was a change of mood amongst civilians and, despite the strenuous efforts of the Nazi propaganda machine, the gloom returned.[15] In Königsberg and in towns throughout Germany the cinemas showed newsreels of guns, tanks, truck, cars and even soldiers sinking into the mud and having to be pulled out. Until the Russian war, newsreels had been very popular but now audiences, which were made up mainly of women and old people, were scared by what they saw. Their fears were deepened as newspaper headlines became gradually more pessimistic.

The drive towards Moscow had started on 2 October 1941 and at first things went so well that Halder confidently predicted, 'With reasonably good direction of battle and moderately good weather we cannot but succeed in encircling Moscow.'[16] But then, on 8 October, the rains had set in, turning the countryside into a quagmire and crippling the German advance; major operations were suspended for the next five weeks. The attack was resumed after the ground had frozen, on 14 November, and, although considerable progress was made, in early December, having reached the outskirts of Moscow, the German Army was confronted by a Soviet force of over 3 million men. Forced into a humiliating retreat, Hitler dismissed the Army Commander-in-Chief, Field Marshal von Brauchitsch, and assumed direct command himself, deciding not only overall strategy on the Russian Front, but day-to-day tactics as well. At about the same time SS *Einsatzgruppen*, supported by the Army, were completing a murderous purge in the territories taken by the Germans. Their victims included 100,000 Jews.

By the end of 1941 the Russians had suffered 4.5 million casualties, and lost 8,000 aircraft and 17,000 tanks. They had lost territory to Germany which contained over half of the Soviet Union's industrial capacity and forty per cent of its population. But the privations of the winter and the loss of half a million of their own men hurt the morale of the Germans much more seriously. The terrible Russian roads had done a huge amount of damage to German road vehicles and tanks; equipment had to be abandoned as vehicles broke down. There were no replacements available for lost vehicles, troops or weapons, and soldiers lacked basic necessities and food. Boots fell to pieces and there were no winter uniforms. This was the result of a decision taken earlier in the year that winter equipment should not be made available since it might give the impression that the Russian war would be a long drawn-out affair.

Events on the Russian Front could not be concealed from German civilians. Stories of the lack of equipment, the chaotic organisation and the terrible suffering filtered through to East Prussia through soldiers invalided home or on leave. In Berlin the authorities were so worried by the possible reaction to the news from the Russian Front that an order went out making it a criminal offence to listen to foreign radio broadcasts. Goebbels warned anyone who listened to the BBC that they risked death or imprisonment. Towards the end of November 1941 everyone in the city received, with their ration-tickets for the month, a little red card, with a hole punched in it which was to be hung on the station dial of a radio set. On the card was the legend 'Racial Comrades! You are Germans! It is your duty not to listen to foreign stations. Those who do so will be mercilessly punished!' A week later many houses were visited by local Nazi officials to make sure that the cards had been fastened to radios and were still there. In the countryside the authorities seemed less fearful and the cards were not distributed – probably because the farming community was regarded as less politically volatile.

On 23 November the *Völkischer Beobachter* had a huge headline 'Rostov Taken', but at Christmas the same news-paper admitted that Rostov, the gateway to the Caucasus, had been evacuated by the German forces and that the Russians had re-possessed the city. Stories were seeping through from the Eastern Front of soldiers being frozen to death at their posts and of train loads arriving at first-aid posts so frost-bitten that limb after limb had to be amputated. It was evident that things were going badly. In Berlin Arvid Fredborg was convinved that an 'atmosphere of catastrophe' had taken hold of the whole German capital.[17] Desperate appeals went out on the radio for gifts for the troops and, at Christmas, children were asked to pack parcels for the soldiers at the front made up of gifts and cheerful letters. They knitted balaclavas, mittens and scarves and made envelopes in which they put dried plants like camomile and peppermint to make tea. Families who did not donate enough had to endure having their houses searched and the contents of their wardrobes taken for the soldiers. It was a particular hardship for civilians to provide these things, for the winter in Germany was also very harsh that year.

Nevertheless, in a radio broadcast Hitler promised that preparations were being made for a new offensive in the spring and his propaganda machine reassured Germans that all was going well on the Eastern Front. From the military point of view the Russians could be counted out; they were, it was said, running out of men and would not be able to continue fighting through the winter and into the following spring.

The winter lull, 1941–2, allowed both sides to rebuild their forces and the Russians completed the process of evacuating industry into the depths of Russia, beyond the Ural Mountains; in the meantime Hitler ordered all nine of his Eastern Front armies to stand firm. In the summer of 1942 the Wehrmacht again took the offensive. Hitler had decided, against the advice of his generals, to abandon any further attempt to take Moscow for the time being and instead to concentrate his forces on the southern section of the Russian Front. He assured the German people that Russia would be annihilated in the next few months. The intention now was to use a plan, code-named Operation Blue, to make for the industrial cities along the Rivers Don and Volga and then to storm Stalingrad before moving on the Caucasus. Hitler had decided that a quick victory at Stalingrad would open up the prospect of sweeping towards the oil fields of the south. Despite warnings of the dangers, which he brushed aside, he declared that the attack would go ahead. Army chiefs were appalled at the prospect of sending their troops into the steppes to face an enemy army fighting for its own land and people. They suspected, as Hitler did not, that in the previous months the Russians had begun to re-equip and had vast forces at their disposal. Stalingrad was deep into enemy territory, was inaccessible across the steppes and difficult to supply; but when Army commanders expressed concern they were dismissed from their posts.

In the spring of 1942 it became clear to Stalin that serious measures would have to be taken to encourage the Russian people to resist. In July 1942, in order to maintain morale and to put pressure on deserters, Stalin issued the historic Order No. 227 'Not a Step Back!'[18] The Red Army was ordered to stand firm against the invader: 'Each position, each metre of Soviet territory must be stubbornly defended to the last drop of blood! We must cling to every inch of Soviet soil and defend it to the end.' If any soldier failed to do this he would be treated as a criminal and a deserter. The notorious NVKD secret police were used to round up alleged cowards, defeatists and saboteurs. No proof of guilt was required and the accused were executed or sent to penal battalions which were sent into the attack ahead of the main army. The Red Army had an extremely successful network of spies to seek out dissidents and a savage code of punishments to deal with them.

Even more importantly, that summer Stalin did something which Hitler was not prepared to do: he handed the day-to-day control of the army and of military strategy back to his generals. Stalin had been so horrified by the defeats of 1941 that he initially decided to try to manage the war personally; in July 1941 he assumed the titles Supreme Commander-in-Chief and Commissar of Defence. However, in August 1942, following the defence of Moscow in the winter of 1941–2, Stalin appointed the successful commander, General Georgi Zhukov, as Deputy Supreme Commander to take charge of the defence of Stalingrad. Zhukov realised that the German attacking force was greatly over-extended and under-resourced. His plans for the defence of Stalingrad were combined with a huge effort to improve overall planning and central direction. The organisation, communication methods and equipment of the Army and Air Force were modernised and new training methods were used. Tanks were built, new airfields were constructed, and radar was installed with the help of the British and Americans.

In 1941, when the German Army rolled into the Soviet Union, a mood of alarm had gripped the Russian people. Many civilians packed what they could into covered *panje* wagons (as the Germans called them) and moved eastwards in a desperate flight from the advancing Germans. Most were convinced that defeat was inevitable but Stalin was not prepared to countenance the prospect of surrender. To try to prevent a recurrence of such panic a propaganda campaign was also started in 1942 to rouse Soviet civilians to put all their efforts into the defence of their country. The Russian people were cajoled and persuaded to put everything they could into the struggle, with the government doing all it could to induce a determination to win what Stalin now called 'the Great Patriotic War'. This resulted in a widespread and spontaneous nationalistic revival and a wave of revulsion against German brutality.

To encourage his people Stalin even overturned many long-held principles of Bolshevism. Churches were reopened after years of religious persecution and Orthodox priests responded by exhorting their congregations to fight for their country. New medals were struck for heroism and officers' uniforms were reinstated; a huge effort was made to restore to the Red Army a sense of self-confidence. Many people who had hitherto been hostile to the Stalinist regime put aside their doubts and showed great willingness to defend their country at all costs. Stalin called on them to turn the whole

Soviet Union into a 'war camp' to save the country from annihilation by the enemy. This was to involve either fighting or working for the defence of Russia.

In Germany, Hitler retained complete control over all military decisions. In the first months of the Second World War Hitler had confounded his military critics with the success of his *Blitzkrieg* strategy and he began to believe in his own infallibility. As a result of Germany's early victories many Army leaders were prepared to accept his views when he first set out his plans for Operation Barbarossa. They only began to express doubts about his strategy when he changed his mind about completing the assault on Moscow in August 1941. Hitler brushed aside their warnings and Guderian's army was ordered to halt its advance on Moscow and switch to the southern front to help with the attack on Kiev. In December 1941 Hitler sacked several top generals, including Fedor von Bock and Guderian, when their opinions contradicted his own. As time went on Hitler's control over military strategy became absolute and, as Richard Overy explains in *Why the Allies Won*:

> The German war became a remarkable one-man show in which intuition displaced rational evaluation and megalomaniac conviction ousted common sense ... Hitler interfered with the smallest details of battles. The consequences were predictable. Instead of an overall strategy, Hitler substituted a jumble of individual decisions and orders. 'There was,' wrote Zeitzler [the Army Chief of Staff from September 1942] 'no delegation of powers or coordinated action ... no decisions on policy'. Even allowing for professional jealousy, the generals' recollections of Hitler's leadership paint a uniform picture of a man quite out of his depth.[19]

Despite the difficulties of the previous winter, as the spring of 1942 came both the Russians and Germans believed that German victory was likely. In just a few weeks the Red Army was driven out of the whole area south of Kharkov and the Crimea was captured. Rostov fell to the Wehrmacht at the end of July. The German high command was still nervous about pushing on to Stalingrad, however. They warned Hitler that there were immense dangers in proceeding so far east: the supply lines were difficult to maintain and would become more so as autumn approached. Hitler would not listen; his orders were that Army Group B, including the Sixth Army and Fourth Panzer Army, was to push on to Stalingrad whilst Army Group A was to split off and make for the eastern Black Sea coast and Grozny in order to secure reliable oil supplies. This decision severely reduced the number of troops available for the attack on Stalingrad.

On 7 August, General Hermann Hoth's Fourth Panzer Army came within thirty kilometres of Stalingrad, and Paulus's Sixth Army arrived to begin the main assault on the city which extended for several kilometres along the east bank of the River Volga. The attack started with a huge aerial bombardment which destroyed most of the outer suburbs and pushed back the Soviets to their middle line of defence.

On 23 August the Germans began a campaign of saturation bombing. Thousands of bombs caused oil-storage tanks to the north of the town centre to explode, resulting in acrid fumes and a sea of fire. Torrents of burning oil and petrol flowed into the Volga until the river itself was in flames. Houses and apartments were engulfed and 40,000 civilian inhabitants, whom the Russians had refused to evacuate, were killed. A thick layer of ash covered the whole area and erupted in clouds of grey dust wherever a new shell fell. Stalingrad became a gigantic pile of ruins and debris stretching along the banks of the Volga.

Hitler was in jubilant mood when he received the news from his generals in early September that they would seize the city and cross the Volga in a few days. But they had not reckoned with the military skills of Zhukhov, who proposed to Stalin a counter-offensive to be launched in the late autumn.

German progress towards the centre of Stalingrad was meanwhile delayed by face-to-face fighting which broke out amidst the debris which had accumulated as a result of their onslaught. The rubble provided easily defensible positions for the Russians, who showed incredible endurance and determination and were able to reduce the battle to house-to-house fighting – a style of combat which the Germans called *Rattenkrieg*, the war of the rats. Both sides ended up taking refuge in the cellars of bombed-out buildings. The German Panzers became entrapped in narrow, rubble-strewn streets which did not allow their crews to take advantage of their superior fighting skills.

Day and night savage hand-to-hand battles raged in the ruined city, often fought with knives, clubs, shovels and even stones. The dead were left where they fell. Civilians trapped in the city cowered in underground shelters, only emerging when there was a lull in the fighting to look for dead horses and dogs and rats and to fill pots and pans with polluted water to feed themselves and their starving children. At night the Russians used knives and bayonets to kill the Germans as they cowered in the cellars and by day they used sniper fire.

For the Russians the ejection of the German Sixth Army from Stalingrad was of desperate importance. They had seen the city, of which they were so proud, collapse into rubble and ashes. General Vasily Chuikov, who had taken over command of the Soviet forces in the city itself in September 1942, had found:

... the streets of the city dead; there is not a single green twig; everything has perished into flames. All that is left of the wooden houses is a pile of ashes and stove chimneys sticking out of them.[20]

Other witnesses described Stalingrad as looking as if it had been the epicentre of a giant earthquake. A layer of thick dust lay over the whole area and in the air hung the acrid fumes of scorched wood and brick and the stench of burning flesh.

By the end of the first week of September 1942 it was clear that the offensive was not cutting through the enemy as fast as promised. Despite renewed efforts, the Russian defence line was not broken and in the meantime the Red Army was laying its preparations for the counter-attack, which would eventually surround the German Sixth Army and bring about its total destruction. Russian soldiers fought with a grim determination to save Stalingrad from annihilation. It was clear that there was no strategic advantage for the Germans in continuing the battle but Hitler insisted that retreat was not an option, declaring 'No power on earth will force us out of Stalingrad.'[21] It was a totally unrealistic prediction. German forces were by now much depleted; they lacked fuel, ammunition and transport and their morale was at rock bottom.

Under conditions of maximum security, the Soviet high command put Zhukov's plans into place. They managed to place five armies to the north of Stalingrad, and two armies to the south, together totalling over a million men, without bringing their manoeuvres to the attention of German headquarters. They also assembled 14,000 heavy guns, 979 tanks and 1,350 aircraft. The Germans had posted Romanian, Hungarian and Italian divisions on the flanks of their advance and these were less well trained and equipped than the

Germans. Only the Romanian units noticed what was brewing but, when they tried to warn the Germans, their concerns were ignored. When the attack finally came on 19 November the Germans were taken completely by surprise. Joachim Wieder, the son of a Lutheran pastor from Silesia, who fought with the Sixth Army, recalled the events of that day:

> The 19th of November will live in my memory as a day of black disaster. At the break of dawn on this gloomy, foggy day in late autumn, during which lashing snowstorms were soon to appear, there began simultaneously with the onset of an extraordinarily hard eastern winter, the catastrophe that had been feared and anxiously anticipated by many. The Russians attacked like lightning from the north and the following day from the east, pressing our entire Sixth Army into an iron vice.[22]

The two Romanian armies were destroyed, leaving big holes in the Wehrmacht's lines. The German XLVIII Panzer Korps put up a fight in the north, but only five days later, on 23 November, the Russian spearhead completed the encirclement of the 300,000 soldiers of the German Sixth Army. With his units in disarray, General Paulus sought permission to pull his troops back. But Hitler wanted them to stay put and from his headquarters in East Prussia he persuaded Hermann Göring to promise that the Luftwaffe would supply the Sixth Army with all the materials it needed. Over the next few days, more Soviet reinforcements arrived and this made a German break-out almost impossible, even if Hitler had been prepared to permit this. The promised relief operation could not be expected to start immediately and in any case the Luftwaffe did not have sufficient transport aircraft and the weather made flying very difficult. The airlift turned out to be a disaster. The Sixth Army needed about 600 tonnes of goods each day but received at most only around 100. With the army running out of supplies and weapons, food rations for the troops were reduced again and again. A catastrophic picture began slowly to emerge and the hungry and desperate troops became depressed and outraged. On many occasions completely superfluous or non-urgent supplies were flown in. Instead of the desperately needed bread and flour, aircraft brought packages of old newspapers or leaflets from the propaganda department. They also dropped such worthless items as spices, neckties, and other things that were of no conceivable use. Many items which might have been of great use, like overcoats, lay around in warehouses in Germany having been extracted from civilians who also desperately needed them.

The men, living in primitive and dirty wooden bunkers, became increasingly despondent. Russian bombs frequently rained down on them and they were under constant artillery fire. Joachim Wieder remembers how 'the heavy thumping of the flak and the thrumming and screaming of the engines provided an infernal accompanying music' to their lives in the bunkers. It was probably the saddest and most desolate place he had ever laid his eyes on:

> A bare, naked steppe landscape with not a bush nor tree nor a village for kilometres around. The loneliness of the eastern expanses was depressing and this eerie feeling was increased by the early fall of darkness. On the heights, above the infamous Rossoshka valley, the men of our divisions lay in trenches and foxholes in the snow, dying of exhaustion and cold, because the steadily shrinking rations of bread and other food issued were no longer sufficient to provide the physical stamina needed to combat frost

and sickness. Only the crows swarming in the endless steppe found enough to eat. These croaking companions of death did very well for themselves.[23]

At last realising how desperate the situation was, Hitler allowed the planning of a 'break-in' to relieve the Sixth Army. In charge of this operation was Field Marshal Erich von Manstein. His task was daunting. He was limited in his freedom to act, and he had few reserves to work with. He finally managed to scrape together eleven divisions for a relief attack, which started on 12 December 1942 and was code-named Winter Storm. It was too little too late. Just before Christmas the expectations and hopes of the besieged Sixth Army collapsed and the relief force was compelled to retreat.

At the end of 1942 the reality of defeat at Stalingrad hung over Germany. Writing in 1942, Howard K. Smith sensed that the Germans wanted an end to the war:

... but they cling to the lion's tail because they are terrorised by the nightmare of what will happen to them if they fail to win the war. They fear what their long-suffering enemies will do to them; of what the tortured people of their enslaved nations, Russia, Poland, Czechoslovakia, will do to them when there is no longer a Gestapo to hold them down.[24]

As the New Year arrived Joachim Wieder described how, 'Jangling frost lay over the Stalingrad pocket and breathed its icy, deadly breath.' The bread ration had been reduced to fifty grams a day and German soldiers were dying of cold and lack of food. Their morale was on the verge of collapse when, on 10 January 1943, the Soviets launched Operation Ring, which cut the Sixth Army in two. Despite the ferocity of the attack, orders came from the Führer's headquarters that no retreat should take place. The decision cost the German

Army dear. Tens of thousands of troops were killed for the sake of holding a line which was ultimately unsustainable. Thousands of kilometres from home, with the troops starving, exhausted, cold and sick, the prolonged fighting was costing thousands of lives to no purpose.

Joachim Wieder records that, in the second half of January, 'In the desolate snowscape of the Don steppe was a tragedy of unimaginable proportions.' German soldiers were lacking food, weapons, rest, warmth, hope: 'In short we were lacking in all the vital conditions for fighting.' Stalingrad itself lay in ruins:

> . . . a desolate city that had bled to death and died from a thousand wounds. For half a year destruction and death had celebrated orgies here and hardly left anything save the torn stumps of houses, naked rows of walls, chimneys sticking up from vast piles of rubble, gutted factories, formless hunks of asphalt.

In these dark days Wieder was forced also to confront the fact that the impending military catastrophe was 'the result of presumptuous beliefs and actions that had shaken the healthy foundations of our intellectual, cultural and national life'. National Socialism had 'unleashed fatal forces' and he could not believe 'that our employment here in Stalingrad was part of a noble or legitimate battle for German interests'.[25]

On 22 January General Paulus asked Hitler's permission to surrender. Hitler refused. He also rejected a request from Manstein that such permission be granted. 'I forbid surrender. The army will hold its position,' he ordered. 'The army is to stand fast to the last soldier and the last bullet.'[26] A week later, on 1 February 1943, Paulus surrendered.

Although Hitler raged and called those who gave in cowards, the battle was over, and the Russian people and military found renewed strength. To many it was the turning point of the war, signalling the eventual end of the Third Reich and with it the obliteration of the city of Königsberg. Two-thirds of the Sixth Army had died in the fighting or through starvation and the cold. The remnants were mostly killed by the Russians after the surrender or sent to labour camps. The Russians had lost nearly half a million men in the defence and recapture of Stalingrad but the Red Army generals were now convinced that, after this, the initiative had passed to them. At long last the German forces had lost their reputation for invincibility.

At home in Germany the news of the surrender at Stalingrad was followed by three days of national mourning. German radio repeatedly played the 'Funeral March' from Wagner's *Götterdammerung* and soon after Goebbels declared that now the country was in a state of 'total war'.[27] Every German would have to be involved in the war effort. Bars, dance halls, shops and restaurants closed in many cities; rations were cut and the streets were deserted. Older men were called up to serve in the Army and for the first time women between the ages of seventeen and fifty were required to work in factories. Marion von Dönhoff was in Berlin staying with friends when news of the surrender was announced: 'When we heard the news on the radio,' she wrote, 'we said with one voice – now the war is lost.'[28] Königsberg shared in the deep gloom and those whose friends and relatives had fought at Stalingrad became more and more pessimistic about the eventual outcome of the war.

After Stalingrad the initiative passed to the Russians. As 1943 began Soviet commanders experimented with a variety of strategic plans and they also came to value the enormous asset they had in their men. Many of the Russian troops were ill-educated and had little preparation for battle but they fought with dogged determination and enormous physical resilience and were able to keep going in icy conditions on slim rations. At Stalingrad the furious Soviet attacks had taken the German military by surprise. 'The number, duration and fury of those attacks exhausted and numbed us completely,' wrote one German soldier. 'Our advance had been an ordinary move on a fairly narrow sector and yet they contested it day after day with masses of men.' It was almost impossible for German troops to deal with such attacks. Blizzards obscured their vision, horses slipped and fell and machine guns failed to work in icy conditions. Harry Mielert wrote about the 'terrible snow storms' which obliterated villages and trails so that it became impossible for the soldiers to orient themselves. 'Every path, every trail is gone within a few minutes ... so here we stand on this front, lonely, without knowing what is to the right or left of us.'[29]

Russian soldiers were not afraid of the harsh winter weather in which their generals often preferred to fight. In many battles Soviet troops took advantage of blizzard conditions to advance on the German lines wearing white uniforms and reached them without being detected. The defence of Moscow took place in December 1941; a year later the campaign to save Stalingrad was launched in November; the invasion of the Ukraine began in December 1943 and the final attack on East Prussia began in January 1945. In his book *War on the Eastern Front*, James Lucas describes how, on occasions:

> Suddenly – and it was always sudden – figures would loom out of the snow – Siberian ski troops appeared, camouflaged in white and inured to sub-zero temperatures. They would sweep across the trench line to spray sentries with bullets from machine pistols or to hurl hand grenades before vanishing into concealing snow clouds, usually before fire could be returned.[30]

German soldiers noticed how well ordinary Russian soldiers coped with difficult terrain – dense forests, swamps, steppes and land covered with deep snow. They also had suitable clothing for the different climates in which they had to fight. They were issued with boots several sizes too large so that they could be stuffed with straw and paper during the coldest weather and later in the war they were equipped with large felt boots, *valenki*, with excellent insulation qualities. The winter overcoat was lined and they wore head-dresses lined with lamb's wool. Russian soldiers were also extremely good at improvisation; they were adept at foraging for food and built themselves shelters very quickly, even in the most inhospitable of terrain. Many Russian infantrymen carried machine pistols which they wore slung around their necks and carried in front of their chests ready for action. They were followed by anti-tank guns which were set up on emplacements which could be established in a very short time. Once the Soviet Army was entrenched, soldiers hung on to their positions with great tenacity and were very hard to move. If they were eventually driven out they would lay waste the countryside as they retreated.

The Russians were proficient at night manoeuvres, shifting into new positions in the hours of darkness. They favoured the use of the dense forests for their approaches since woods gave an enormous amount of cover, particularly at night. They also frequently fortified forest positions in such a way as to make them impenetrable. These garrisons were very difficult for the Germans to attack and caused many casualties. A common tactic was to use the outskirts of a wood or forest as the starting point for a major attack. Wave upon wave of men would surge out of the forests.[31]

The Red Army was also very adept in the use of deceptions and subterfuge. Diversionary attacks were frequently launched to switch German attention from the main strike and sometimes dummy smoke screens were used as a way of deflecting enemy fire. Before an offensive started the Russians often used tactics to mislead the Germans about the time and place of the intended attack. On one occasion they were found to have been running motor engines at night to create the impression that tanks and other vehicles were on the move.[32]

After the surrender at Stalingrad the German Army in the east was heavily depleted. In February 1943 the Russians recaptured Rostov but Hitler was not prepared to give in. He desperately needed a victory in order to regain the initiative on the Eastern Front and to 'avenge the humiliation of Stalingrad. In the spring the Russians received secret warnings that the German Army was building up huge forces at Kursk. Stalin was keen to launch a pre-emptive strike but General Zhukhov restrained him and insisted on letting the Germans attack first, predicting that they would wear themselves out on the massive defences he had put in place. Helped by local civilians, the Russian troops laid an enormous array of tank traps, minefields and anti-tank guns. The minefields were specially designed to channel armoured formations into anti-tank defences which were intended to cause massive German losses. The Soviet Army had at the ready forty per cent of its total manpower and seventy-five per cent of its available armaments.

Fighting began on 5 July 1943 and, after a week of furious tank battles, it became clear that German losses were so great that they could not win. Within a few days more they were in retreat and Hitler was never to regain the land he had lost.[33] Despite the symbolism of the surrender at Stalingrad the defeat at Kursk was probably the real turning point in the war.

After the battle for Kursk the strength and effectiveness of the German armies entered a period of almost constant decline. As General Alfred Jodl, Hitler's deputy chief of staff, put it, 'It was clear, not only to the responsible soldiers but to Hitler too, that the God of War had now turned from Germany and gone over to the other camp.'[34]

To the ordinary German soldiers, defeat now seemed to be inevitable. Guy Sajer, who had fought at Stalingrad, records how in 1943 he and his fellow soldiers:

> ... became heroes without glory. We no longer fought for Hitler, or for National Socialism, or the Third Reich – or even for our fiancées or mothers or families trapped in bomb-ravaged towns. We fought from simple fear, which was our motivating power. We fought for ourselves, so that we wouldn't die in holes filled with mud and snow; we fought like rats.[35]

By the end of 1943 the German high command had no illusions about the eventual outcome of the war. The Red Army had regained a vast area of Russia, even though the scorched-earth tactics of the retreating Wehrmacht had rendered most of it useless, and its forward march seemed unstoppable. As Guy Sajer so aptly says:

> There is no sepulchre for the Germans killed in Russia [but simply] a profound sense of hopelessness and misery. More scorched earth and weeks of terror; more hands cracked open by chilblains; and more fatal acceptance of the idea of death.[36]

Between December 1943 and March 1944 the Red Army successfully freed Leningrad, the Ukraine, the Crimea and the eastern part of Belorussia; the German struggle to hold them back proved hopeless. In March 1944 the Red Army reached the borders of Poland, and Russian progress along the whole front was so relentless that, by the middle of 1944, they had reached the East Prussian border. Despite insistence from both the government and the military leadership that 'as long as a single German soldier remains alive no Bolshevik will tread on German soil' the invasion of East Prussia was now inevitable. As each German-occupied territory was regained, Russian citizens who were believed to have collaborated with the Germans were severely punished by the advancing Red Army.

By mid-1944 the Germans were in retreat everywhere and in particular were struggling to shore up their forces on the Eastern Front. Most of their units were reduced to two-thirds or less of their original strength and those recruits who could be found were poorly trained and suffered an abnormally high casualty rate. As a result of the combination of superior Russian strategic planning and Hitler's incompetence, a vast area of central Russia had been recaptured, although much of it was so devastated it would take years for it to recover from the German invasion. There was apparently no strategy in place to organise an effective and safe German retreat. Gottlob Bidermann came to realise that:

> The Wehrmacht had never fully developed or learned the tactics and methods of retreat. The German soldier was taught to view retreat solely as defeat, with no advantages forthcoming. [As a result] the collapse of Army Group Centre resulted in chaos. This was clearly exhibited by the countless units observed on the roads and bridges fleeing to the rear, seemingly leaderless and without direction. Some battered units were overcome with panic, and they streamed towards the west on foot and in vehicles of every description. The confusion, the panic-stricken soldiers, the jamming of all movements along the passable roads would earlier have been considered an inconceivable scenario, but the collapse of discipline and order had become a reality.

As they retreated they were constantly harassed by Russian attacks:

> The Russians were able to increase the turmoil and confusion through constant attacks with their air force which bombed and strafed all roadways and rail lines, leaving shattered, demoralised fragments of once proud regiments strewn in their path ... And the highest commander, to whom credit for the catastrophe should be awarded, was not present to witness what his decisions had wrought. As always, the soldiers in the field bore the brunt of these mistakes and paid with their lives.[37]

The last phase of the war, from the beginning of 1944 to May 1945 showed Soviet military strategy at its best. The need to plan effectively was increased by a manpower crisis which made it impossible for the Soviet Army to continue to throw soldiers into battle with little regard as to whether or not they survived. Now planning an offensive in detail was essential – from the deployment of reconnaissance troops before an attack began to the timing of the use of artillery, tanks and aircraft.

The lives of the retreating German troops became increasingly difficult. Guy Sajer recalls how his unit received only about one-tenth of the supplies it needed and was:

> ... obliged to live off the local inhabitants, who were very hard-pressed themselves and more than reluctant in their attitude toward us. The problem of food had become extremely serious. [He and his comrades] seemed to be wandering endlessly toward new horizons on which we never had time to gaze, through an over-sized, over-intense spring, which would not allow us to forget that we were at war. We wanted the

war to stop and dreamed of peace, like the seriously ill
for whom the first sight of spring buds kindles a spark
of life.[38]

On 20 July 1944, a month after the Soviet Army had
launched the campaign which was eventually to expel the
Germans of East Prussia from their homeland, a group of
mainly Prussian officers attempted to assassinate Adolf Hitler
in the *Wolfsschanze*. Prussians were well represented in the
German opposition to Hitler; two-thirds of the plotters were
Prussian, including several aristocrats and many officers of
Infantry Regiment 9, whose swearing-in ceremony had
always carefully avoided Nazi themes such as the singing of
the *Horst Wessel Song* after the national anthem. Gottlob
Bidermann, who was with the retreating army, heard the
news of the failed plot. He feared that:

> The knowledge that a number of our most talented
> and trusted military leaders would attempt to kill our
> head of state proved to us that militarily we could not
> win against the massed, combined might of the allies.

He also recalls how, following the assassination attempt,
the traditional military salute was changed to the Nazi salute.
This was much resented by the soldiers and, as a
consequence:

> Following the order it was not uncommon to observe
> entire companies carrying their mess tins in their right
> hands to avoid being compelled to demonstrate their
> loyalty to the Party.[39]

Hitler took terrible revenge against the plotters and those
suspected of associating with them but it was too late to
restore people's faith in him. Despite living in an atmosphere
of suspicion and terror, most Germans now wanted the war to

come to an end. Amongst civilians the Nazi greeting 'Heil Hitler' grew unpopular and was rarely used, and in private many hoped that the Americans would arrive in time both to liberate them from the Nazis and to prevent a Russian invasion.

Chapter Nine

THE TIME FOR REPAYMENT

Although the Atlantic Charter of 1941 agreed by the President Roosevelt and Prime Minister Churchill had included a commitment to 'oppose territorial changes that do not accord with the freely expressed wishes of the peoples concerned', in March 1943 President Roosevelt and British Foreign Secretary Anthony Eden spoke for the first time officially about the fate of East Prussia. Germany's post-war future had been under discussion since 1941 and became more urgent after the Stalingrad surrender. The most significant outcome of the discussions had been that, to end the war Germany would be expected to surrender unconditionally and would then be divided into zones of occupation, each one occupied by one of the victorious allies. Military occupation was considered an essential instrument for securing total German submission and disarmament and would also demonstrate to the German people the finality of their defeat. 'Total surrender' would be the price of peace.

Stalin's determination to hang on to the areas of eastern Poland he had invaded in 1939 and planned to re-take from Germany was an embarrassment for Britain, which had gone into the war in order to defend the Polish nation. The inter-Allied Teheran Conference of November 1943 concerned itself with the question of Poland's post-war frontiers. Not wanting to fall out with Stalin, Churchill and Roosevelt were conciliatory. It was tacitly agreed that 'what Poland lost in the east she might gain in the west'. As Alfred M. de Zayas says, 'The Western Allies preferred to compensate Poland at the expense of the common enemy – Germany,'[1] but they were also prepared 'to place Poland on wheels' and push the country's borders farther to the west in order to allow Stalin to keep what he wanted.

At first there had been some discussion about the possibility of complete dismemberment of Germany into five separate states, but this was eventually discarded. In the end the question narrowed down to the fate of the eastern side of the Reich. It was agreed that East Prussia and Memel should be permanently confiscated at the end of the war; Poland would keep West Prussia, Pomerania, Upper and Lower Silesia and a slice of Brandenburg, and the Rivers Oder and Neisse would mark the border between Poland and Germany. The Soviets would keep the eastern provinces of Poland that they had taken in 1939. In compensation Poland would get the southern half of East Prussia but the district around Königsberg would go to the Soviet Union, thus giving Russia access to an ice-free port on the Baltic (Pillau/Baltiysk). The native East Prussians, who had been there for 700 years, would be moved out.

Churchill made it sound very straightforward: 'A clean sweep will be made. I am not alarmed by the prospect of the disentanglement of populations, nor even by large transferences.'[2] Confident that the transfer could be humane and orderly, he did not foresee the chaos that was eventually to ensue. At the beginning of 1944 the military situation reinforced Churchill's opinions. Writing to Eden he said,

'The Russians may very soon be in physical possession of these territories and it is absolutely certain that we should never attempt to turn them out.'

Six months later the USA confirmed that, 'The Government should not oppose the annexation by Poland of East Prussia, Danzig and Upper Silesia.' In March 1944 the Earl of Mansfield made it clear to the House of Lords that 'the Atlantic Charter will not apply to Germany',[3] and the outline of the occupation zones was agreed towards the end of the year. Early in 1945, after visiting Stalin in Moscow in October 1944, Churchill conceded that the area of East Prussia to be ceded to Poland would be 'south of Königsberg',[4] implying that the district of Königsberg, with the Baltic port of Pillau, would become part of the Soviet Union.

At what point Hitler knew of these plans is uncertain. Admiral Karl Dönitz, who briefly took over as leader of Germany after Hitler committed suicide, claims in his memoirs that the German government only learnt about them in January 1945. It was then it obtained possession of a copy of the British Operation Order Eclipse which outlined the plans and preparatory measures to be taken for the occupation of Germany by the Soviet Union, the USA and Great Britain.[5]

In February 1945 the 'Big Three' met at Yalta in the Crimea and in a packed agenda discussed the future of Poland. With the Red Army by now occupying most of eastern Europe it was again conceded that the Soviet Union should get Königsberg and it was acknowledged that Stalin also wished to keep Lvov. In return it was agreed that Poland should be shifted west to the Rivers Oder and Neisse and that its territory should include Stettin and Breslau in compensation.

The people of East Prussia and Königsberg certainly had no idea of the fate that awaited them and many of those forced to flee the Russians, even whilst the Yalta Conference was in session, expected to return when the war was over. But the stark truth was that, as the end of the war approached, the terrible sufferings of the Jews, the Poles and the Russians were to be avenged in the province and its capital. The deaths brought about by the Nazis were uncountable but 2 million East Prussians were to die and 3 million were to lose their homes. As Guido Knopp has said:

> It was the time for repayment for torment and suffering, for the burnt-out villages, destroyed towns, churches and schools; for the arrests, camps and destruction, for Auschwitz, Treblinka, for the extermination camps.[6]

And as de Zayas puts it:

> It was simply the unspeakable inhumanity of Hitler's regime that made Roosevelt and Churchill morally insensitive to what might happen to millions of Germans in the East. The odour of Belsen and Buchenwald was in the air.[7]

Yet, at the end of 1943, the people of Königsberg and East Prussia still clung to the belief that Germany could win the war. Incessant propaganda kept the hope of victory alive and, despite the speed of the Russian advance, many civilians believed government promises that the frontiers of Germany would be defended and kept secure. Domestically, life was still bearable; food was rationed but in this rural province there was plenty milk, potatoes and vegetables. The trams and trains still ran and, although there were constant news reports of air raids in the western part of the country, particularly in the Ruhr, in Königsberg all remained peaceful. Leaving war-damaged Berlin to travel east, Marianne Mackinnon noticed how 'sane and peaceful' the rural areas still appeared:

Trees lined the country roads. A few scattered farms
poked through the flatness of the land. Long strips of
beet and potato crops adjoined miles of corn that stood
golden, high and heavy. Hedges looked as if they had
been embroidered with crimson, dark pinks or ripe
yellows; rooks were swooping low over the fields;
swallows seemed to fall from and immediately surge
back into a sky where the sun had reached its zenith.[8]

However, those who were thoughtful could not avoid
dwelling on the fact that their town was filling with refugees
arriving from the bomb-damaged west, and there were also
foreign workers and soldiers awaiting despatch to the Eastern
Front. Medical and nursing staff also passed through the city
on their way to the front, whilst many thousands of badly
wounded soldiers arrived on their way to hospitals in the
west. Many of these were suffering with severe frostbite for it
was yet another very cold winter. Cinema newsreels showed
German soldiers on the Russian Front dressed up like
mummies, with ice hanging on their beards, eyebrows and on
the openings of their balaclavas. There was, however, no
official information about how the war was going.

One thing was clear: the shelters and underground bunkers
which were under construction were not simply a precaution.

Christmas 1943 was a hard time everywhere for civilians.
The people of Königsberg watched in dismay as they saw
newsreels of bombing raids on German cities which
continued to destroy, disrupt, paralyse and demoralise. Every
day families received news of the deaths and injuries of
young soldiers in the Soviet Union. They heard from
relatives in the west who wrote about houses being blown up
and their occupants buried under rubble, suffocated,
incinerated, widowed and orphaned. Rations were cut again
and rumours of impending defeat now began to grow.

In February 1943 the mobilisation of young boys for the war effort had begun. Youngsters born in 1926 and 1927 were called up to serve in Flak batteries to help defend against air attacks; they wore grey uniforms with a swastika armband and lived in barracks locally, where they continued to receive a basic education from teachers who were not fit for military service. In Königsberg and the rest of East Prussia it was more common for lads to be asked to give support to the Navy and Air Force; many were sent to naval barracks on the coast at places such as Pillau and Memel where they were given dark blue naval uniforms with a gold armband embellished with the word *Marinehelfe*. In Pillau the young recruits went to school each afternoon in the town – and the amount of time they spent at school was reduced as German fortunes in the war fell and the Soviet Army came ever nearer.

Although many in the region expressed worries about the way the war was going, others were still unwisely optimistic and believed the official line that the Russians would never get as far as Germany. They continued to be confident in the New Year despite the fact that, in January 1944, Russian armies freed Leningrad, attacked the German Army in the Ukraine and launched an assault in the Crimea.

In January 1944 recruitment to the Flak batteries and the *Marinehelfer* was extended to boys born in 1928. Martin Bergau was called up to go to Pillau, but when he got there was told that he had been assigned to Flak Battery 201 in Königsberg where his unit's task would be to support the Luftwaffe.[9] The training in anti-aircraft weapons was detailed and challenging for the boys and once it was complete his unit was moved to the border town of Tilsit – which was soon to find itself on the battlefront – and then back again to Königsberg, to Flak Battery 223, which was stationed at Gross Friedrichsberg, Gauleiter Erich Koch's estate, when the full-scale Russian attack was launched.

On 25 June 1944, just three weeks after the D-Day landings in Normandy, the Russians launched a huge offensive along the central part of the Eastern Front. It was Operation Bagration, named after a top commander of the Russian Army fighting Napoleon's forces in the campaign of 1812. The Russians were intent on revenge; they had already driven the Germans out of Greater Russia and were ready to carry the war into south-east Europe and central Poland. As the German war effort faltered the Red Army was ready with huge reserves of men and armaments.

The main Russian attack was aimed at the German Army Group Centre in Belorussia where a Russian army of over two and a half million men faced a depleted German force of half a million men. The attack involved four fronts, or army groups: three Belorussian fronts driving westwards towards East Prussia, Poland and Lithuania and one Baltic front thrusting across and down towards Estonia and Latvia. The Russians had 166 army divisions, consisting of 1,254,300 men, 30,000 guns and mortars, 4,000 tanks, 44,000 machine guns and 6,000 aircraft. The Germans had little chance against such forces but Hitler refused to sanction any withdrawals. Attacks began on the night of 20/21 June 1944. After a catastrophic defeat in which Army Group Centre lost 350,000 men, more than had been lost at Stalingrad, and with a further 57,000 taken as prisoners of war, the Red Army retook Minsk on 2 July, securing the city in an attack that lasted just one morning. They took the rest of Belorussia a few days later. Most of Lithuania was retaken by 13 July 1944.[10]

A year earlier Himmler had issued orders about what should be done if the Wehrmacht ever had to withdraw from the Soviet Union:

> Not a human being, not a single head of cattle, not a kilogram of crops and not a railway line is to remain

behind. Not a house is to remain standing, not a mine is to be available which is not destroyed and not a well which is not poisoned.

Such was the rush to get away that a deliberate scorched-earth policy was hard to put into practice but troops obeyed Himmler's orders where they could. Some damage was in fact almost inevitable. In 1944 the German retreat had become so disorganised that soldiers had to rely on their own ingenuity to find food. Villages were stripped of anything that was of use to the retreating army and men were prepared to use any tactic to get hold of food. Many villages were totally destroyed and their inhabitants killed or left for dead. As a result, as they advanced, the Russians found parts of the countryside ruined and villages put to the torch. If the people of East Prussia had known what the Wehrmacht had done they might have thought about taking flight in the summer of 1944.

The first signs of what was to come occurred in June, when frequent reconnaissance flights took place over the city of Königsberg, which led to the sirens going off. Air-raid practice had been going on for some weeks and the townsfolk rushed to the shelters where they were looked after by students who had trained as civilian helpers (*Laienhelferin*). Fearing things would get worse, some left the city whilst others arranged to have their valuables moved to the country. Gauleiter Koch ordered all women under fifty to go to work unless they had children of school age and all school children over the age of sixteen had to leave and work too. All were to 'take up arms' (*Volksaufgebot in Waffen*) to save the homeland. The Königsberg University authorities decided that the length of terms would be increased in order that students should graduate more quickly.

Arno Surminski who grew up near Rastenburg, recalled the shock of realising that the war was now on their doorsteps.

'We had a very peaceful time in the war. We only heard about the war from travellers from the front.' Far away from the bombers, the people of East Prussia had been lulled by the propaganda of the regime that the enemy would not be able to get as far as Königsberg. The land of amber, of dark woods and crystal lakes; the land of high skies and storks:

> ... had always seemed like a refuge for the bombed-out people of other parts of the Reich, but as the storks left that winter everyone said the same thing as they watched them leave 'Yes, off they go; and us, what will happen to us?'[11]

Marion von Dönhoff had been one of the few who foresaw what was likely to happen. When the Russian Campaign failed in 1943 she realised that one day East Prussia would be lost. She recalls how, though she still had changes and improvements made on her Friedrichstein estate in the last years of the war, she would also say, 'The Russians will be pleased when they see this.' She had been waiting to say her final farewells for months.[12]

The destruction of the city of Königsberg began not with the Russians but with two devastating aerial attacks by British bombers on the nights of 26/27 and 29/30 August 1944. Only two weeks previously the Albertina University had celebrated its 400th anniversary and had accepted three new statues from Gauleiter Koch – of Kant, Copernicus and Hitler. The sirens had been going off nightly for some weeks but the attacks, when they came, took the inhabitants completely by surprise. Königsberg was not of great strategic importance but as part of the policy to lower civilian morale through aerial bombing, and to give support to the Russian campaign on the Eastern Front, British Lancaster bombers flew over the city that August, dropping 500 tons of bombs on the first night. Although Königsberg had few air defences in this first attack the inner city got off relatively lightly, although many were killed in the suburbs.

On the second occasion, 179 RAF Lancaster bombers returned, this time using a greater weight of incendiary bombs. These destroyed most buildings in the Königstrasse, Rossgärter and large parts of the city centre, including the Kneiphof Island. The Cathedral was reduced to a shell, as was the old Castle. All five bridges connecting the Kneiphof to the city were destroyed and people were trapped on the Island. Some jumped into the river with their clothes in flames. Onlookers recall how everything seemed to be on fire; houses collapsed and blocked the roads and the city burned all day and the next night. Civilians living in the narrow streets of the Altstadt had very little hope of escaping. They were incinerated in the cellars and in the streets in front of their houses.

In the aftermath people wandered about badly burnt, carrying children with scorched clothes, and looking for doctors or hospitals. They wept as they described people being burnt or suffocated in their houses or cellars, and spoke of a firestorm that was so tremendous that it sucked people into the flames. Some of the dead were left naked because the firestorm had pulled off their clothes.

Huge craters appeared in the streets and the trams stopped running because the tramlines were destroyed. The town was unrecognisable. By the Pregel not one of the old warehouses in the Speicher district was left standing. Most of the University was in ruins. The Hauptbahnhof was filled with bodies, as were the trains that stopped there. All that was left were the suburbs to the north of the Pregel (Hufen and Ratshof) and, to the south of the city, Amalienlau, Juditten and the workers' suburb of Ponarth. Large diggers had to be used to make mass graves in the town cemeteries. Nearly 200,000 people had been made homeless and an estimated

4,000 had been killed, though the dead were never properly counted. Over fifty per cent of the city's historic buildings and their irreplaceable contents had been destroyed. The thousands made homeless moved into the city parks with the few possessions they had managed to save; they were covered with soot and their clothes were often burnt. For almost three days no one could enter the city, and even after the flames died down the stones and ground remained untouchable. A huge cloud of smoke 'as broad and tall as the mountain of smoke from later atom bomb explosions' hung over the city and the smoke and the stench of incinerated bodies lasted for weeks. Special troops gathered the incinerated corpses lying in the streets or suffocated in their cellars.[13]

Werner Terpitz was just fifteen when the bombs fell. Like many youngsters of his age from the countryside, he lived in lodgings in the city whilst attending grammar school. He remembers how:

> On the evening of 29 August the attack was renewed, more aircraft and more bombs. All men were ordered out of the shelters to help. I hesitated; was I a man or a boy? In the end I joined the men and went out and saw the burning streets and thought I was having a terrible dream. It looked like a deserted hell; windows stood wide open, the church and our house were on fire. I began to clear the house and some of the others. Everyone bundled things up and dragged them outside. Escaping to the bridge, I looked at the surroundings. Everything was on fire, our things, our church, our school, and the house of my violin teacher, my violin, even the sack of blackberries, which we had just gathered. Everything I had ever owned was now ashes.[14]

The bombing of Königsberg was only given a brief mention in the German national news but no one who lived nearby was in any doubt about the seriousness of the raids. The glow of the fires on the horizon could be seen from kilometres around and Werner's parents saw the flames from their home a hundred kilometres to the east. Fine ash and scraps of paper were blown through the air and the city was blanketed with burning fibres which rained down on the ruins. In the fields farmers found burnt-out wrecks of aircraft and rubble, the results of the air battle over Königsberg. The East Prussians no longer felt immune from the war; retribution had begun.

Michael Wieck, who had 'watched helplessly as the flames greedily devoured venerable old Königsberg', recalls that it was several days before the heat of the incendiary bombs had diminished enough for people to walk through the streets again and that, 'The entire city was a danger zone, everywhere buildings were on the brink of collapse.' He mocked the Party organisations who represented themselves as heroes in the hour of need:

> ... dispensing blankets, coffee and words of comfort; an hour of need that they themselves had provoked ... The air raid on Königsberg served as a notice of its impending destruction ... and began the death of a city that lost forever what had made it what it was. The refusal to bring a war already lost to a timely end and to destroy a dictatorship squandered away the last chance for East Prussia. [Nevertheless] although I longed for Hitler's defeat we mourned the fate of Königsberg from the depths of our souls.[15]

Dora Skopp's father found his furrier's shop had been completely destroyed. As father and daughter reached the Altstadt:

The effects of the destruction were indescribable. In the Altstadt, behind the Schmiederstrasse, we could see no trace of the old narrow lanes – just mounds of rubble, some over a metre high. All that remained of father's shop was a single steel girder. All the houses from the Munchhof to the New Market were burnt out and the whole castle complex was a sad ruin – a symbol of death.[16]

So many of the city's bridges had been damaged that the Kneiphof could only be reached by boat. Nearly all the buildings there were burnt to the ground, their end hastened by the old timbers which provided the framework of most. The fourteenth-century cathedral was in ruins and its many treasures were lost. The Island was uninhabitable and remained almost deserted for the rest of the war.

However, the British attack did not dent morale permanently; the people simply picked themselves up and tried to make the best of things. Soon afterwards the main roads were cleared, leaving the rubble on the side, often covering the pavements. Water and electricity were restored; the shops opened again; and trams and trains started running again. The cinemas re-opened, showing *Heimatfilme* – cheery German musicals and romantic comedies with predictably happy endings. Girls in dirndls were courted by handsome Aryan heroes. 'Morale would not be so high without the cinema' was a commonly expressed belief and the films often worked their magic, allowing Königsbergers a couple of hours of escape from the reality of their damaged city. The Hauptbahnhof opened again, without its roof, with the tickets being sold from a little wooden hut. However, some families, sensing that this was the beginning of the end, made the decision to leave the city and some women and children were evacuated to Saxony and Thuringia.[17]

After the air raids on Königsberg and the inroads of the Red Army, General Friedrich Hosbach, commander of the German Fourth Army, had suggested the preventative evacuation of the eastern areas of the province. The response from Hitler was unequivocal: not one inch of German soil would be sacrificed and the people must be prepared to fight 'to the last man and to the last round'. Gauleiter Koch was equally opposed to evacuation. It would, he declared, look like defeatism; everyone must stay and defend their homeland.

Trapped and powerless in Kurland (Courland) far to the north of Königsberg, German Army Group North was not allowed to evacuate by sea. Hitler wanted to leave it there to act as the basis for a renewed attack in the spring. Gottlob Bidermann served with the 132nd Infantry Division in Army Group North:

> Thus [the division] stood to the bitter end on the last front. We were resolved never to surrender, and the troops in Kurland were to bear the ominous distinction of being the only combat units of the German Army that were never defeated in open battle.

Bidermann was well aware how badly equipped German forces were. He recalls that ammunition was so scarce that artillery batteries were only allotted two rations of shells a day, machine guns were permitted to fire only in semi-automatic mode and 'firing entire belts was allowed only when repelling an attack'. Petrol and food were also in short supply: 'Resourceful drivers always held a few carefully hidden canisters of fuel in reserve and an extra sack of barley or dried rhubarb was always put aside for the horses.' The death rate among the horses was high from shrapnel wounds and as a result 'the cooks learned to prepare baked horse liver with onions' and horsemeat goulash was a welcome respite to the soldiers meagre diet. At the end of September 1944 their sector remained 'ominously quiet' but in mid-October Russian tanks appeared at Polangen to the north of Memel and they were reminded of the dangers that awaited them. Towards the end of October a 'desperate plan had been conceived' to break out of the pocket but before it could be put into action the Soviets had attacked with such ferocity that the plan could not be implemented.[18]

Goebbels belatedly set himself the task of recruiting an extra million men to reinforce the army by what many regarded as scraping the bottom of the barrel. The new recruits were the old, the sick or those in reserved occupations who had previously been considered too valuable elsewhere; they were speedily recruited and dispatched half-trained and ill-equipped to the front. In a speech on 18 October, which clearly revealed that he had lost all sense of reality, Hitler declared:

> While the adversary believes that it is going to make the final onslaught we are determined to carry out the second great action of our people. With our great strength we will succeed, just as we did in 1939 and 1940, in not only breaking the destructive designs of the enemy but also in pushing them back so far from the Reich that the future of Germany will be secure.

A few days earlier Himmler, already head of the SS and its secret police section the Gestapo, overlord of the armaments industry and organiser of thirty-eight Waffen-SS divisions had been made commander of the Replacement Army, which prepared reinforcements for all the fighting fronts. Virtually every division was severely under-strength in terms both of men and equipment, and shortages of raw materials made it increasingly difficult to produce tanks, aircraft or even trucks. The loss of Romania and the frequent Allied bombing attacks on synthetic fuel plants had also seriously reduced available fuel. By calling up any man under sixty who was able to fight Himmler raised 500,000 men who were sent to the front with little training and little equipment.

Martin Bormann, Hitler's secretary, began the recruitment of a home guard. The *Deutscher Volkssturm* was constituted on 25 September 1944 'by order of the Führer'. Hitler publicly announced its formation in his speech of 18 October. It was intended 'to strengthen the active forces of our Wehrmacht and especially to conduct inexorable fighting at all places where the enemy intends to set foot on German soil'. On 19 October a decree was published from Hitler that the Volkssturm would be formed from all men aged sixteen to sixty who were capable of bearing arms. 'The Volkssturm today', Himmler declared optimistically 'has the task of engaging the enemy with fanaticism and if possible wiping him out.'

The truth was that in the previous few years the male population had been combed through several times in search of final reserves and those who were fit enough were already fighting at the front. The Reich was now forced to rely for its final defence on young members of the Hitler Youth who had been trained to prepare for self-sacrifice for the Führer and would now be conscripted into the Volkssturm. The plan was that a 6-million-strong force would have 19,180 battalions.[19]

Since Hitler had lost trust in the Army, the order was given that the Volkssturm was not to co-operate or to serve under Army leadership but would be rallied and receive orders directly from him or his appointed representatives, the Gauleiters. Leaders of the Volkssturm units were as far as possible to be 'reliable and resolute National Socialists' ideally with some front-line experience. The tasks of the Volkssturm were to seek out and destroy agents and small sabotage groups, to guard bridges, streets and key buildings, to reinforce depleted Army units, to plug gaps in the front and to crush feared uprisings by prisoners of war and foreign workers. There was to be no pay except when engaged in fighting. Not all the intended battalions were formed but about 700 did see combat, mostly along Germany's Eastern Front against the Russians. All members of the Volkssturm were classed as soldiers under the Army code for their duration of service, which was to take place locally whenever an area was threatened. In addition to providing extra manpower, albeit not very efficient, there was the added advantage that a large proportion of the male population who had not previously fought were now under military control. This would help prevent the kind of civilian unrest which had marked the final months of the First World War and contributed to the German surrender.

The units were formed with a desperate haste; equipment was now so lacking that recruits had to provide their own clothing, kit, rucksack and blankets. Weapons were also in very short supply and for many there were not even identifying armbands. This broke the requirements of the Geneva Convention and laid recruits open to the charge of being terrorists if they were captured. The Volkssturm was, in the main, badly led by inexperienced officers; often they were out-of-condition middle-aged civilians who had not previously been considered fit to serve in the armed forces. The recruits, many of whom were already working a seventy-two-hour 'war emergency' week, were given a forty-eight-hour training programme to ready them for their appointed tasks. Often entire Hitler Youth groups enlisted together, for anyone who failed to volunteer was labelled a coward. Fed by Nazi propaganda, they were determined to fight to the last to defend both the Third Reich and their own families. A spectacular colour film, *Kolberg*, was made which aimed to impress the young. Its subject was the glorious stand made by the citizens of Kolberg in Pomerania against a besieging

French army during the Napoleonic Wars and it was full of resounding phrases such as 'You have a duty to defend or die' and 'There is always pain in bringing forth greatness'. The fighting ability of the Volkssturm units was poor. Lacking adequate weapons, ammunition and training, their morale was low and the desertion rate was high. Most of the reluctant recruits to the Volkssturm regarded the whole exercise as pointless. A popular poem doing the rounds in East Prussia made their feelings clear:

> I'm about to taste revenge and retribution
> By joining up dear Klaus.
> You are 16 and I am 66
> And we almost look like real men
> We're called the ragged saviours
> And march happily behind Hitler's staff.
> Mice and men and bag and baggage
> We follow him to our grave.

Helmut Altner, who was called up to the Volkssturm in the spring of 1945, was given his uniform in great haste:

> The individual items are thrown at us after a quick appraisal of the figure. 'OK? Out!' It is only when we get back to our barrack room that we can really see things properly. My jacket is too big and flaps around my body, the sleeves reaching down to my fingertips. On the other hand the trousers barely reach my knees and the boots pinch. 'OK?' I am not the only one. Most of my comrades look either as if they are scarecrows or wearing their first school uniforms.[20]

Marion von Dönhoff remembers the day in her village of Quittainen near Königsberg when an order came from the mayor to all men not in the Army that they must join the Volkssturm. Apart from a few who had particular jobs the

order applied to all, even sixteen-year-olds and some
invalids:

> A great lament began in the village. They all hobbled
> out; lame Marx, half-blind Katter, old Hinz, all
> accompanied by their crying wives. The mayor gave
> them Italian muskets and each got 18 cartridges.
> Nothing else was available . . . And then they were
> turned out into the freezing winter night to await their
> fate.[21]

The Gauleiters were given the authority to call up the
Volkssturm. Koch seized on the idea with alacrity. He refused
to put the Volkssturm under military command and even
confiscated weapons and equipment which were supposed to
go to the Army to give to the Volkssturm. He decided that in
Königsberg the Volkssturm would be used to carry out a plan
floated by Himmler earlier in the year to build an Eastern
Wall to keep the Russians out. With a call to loyalty and a
passionate demand that help was needed to defend the
Führer and the Fatherland, the citizens of Königsberg must
voluntarily find 100,000 people to defend East Prussia. In
reality 100,000 volunteers fit enough to do the work were not
available; draconian measures had to be used to get people to
leave their jobs and build the defences.

Otto Schneidereit, who lived on the most easterly frontier
of East Prussia, had been called up in August 1944 to help
with preparing defences. The battlefront was getting closer
and closer. Taken by train to Schirwindt, the smallest frontier
town in East Prussia, he was ordered to help organise a
thousand members of the Hitler Youth who were to start
constructing the Eastern Wall against the rapidly advancing
Soviet Army. They worked for several weeks until the news
came that, despite their labours, the Russians had broken
through. Schneidereit eventually returned to his parent's

home in Haselberg in October 1944 to find that the
breakthrough had indeed occurred and that they were
preparing for evacuation. Nevertheless the 'Erich Koch Wall'
had been built and Koch reported to his leader 'The first
battalion is in place,' even though it was not clear who would
be there to defend it when the Russians arrived.[22]
Koch knew only too well what was likely to happen when
the Russians invaded East Prussia. In 1943 he had been
appointed Reichskommissar for the Ukraine and maintained
a regime characterised by forced labour, hunger and
shootings. Countless Russian prisoners had been killed.
Civilians had been murdered, towns and villages destroyed.

Hans Graf von Lehndorff, in his *East Prussian Diary*
recollects that he felt the first foreboding of catastrophe in
the final days of June 1944. It crept up slowly:

> ... the realisation that one day we would have to leave
> our sun-drenched land. And then the roads were
> packed with refugees from Lithuania and stray cattle
> wandered on our fields, and we knew that we would
> soon have to follow the push to the west. It was hard to
> take it in at first, but as summer faded and the storks
> prepared to migrate it became clear to us that what we
> had tried so hard to ignore could no longer be put out of
> our minds. In the villages there were people every-
> where staring up into the sky watching as the great
> birds left, realising that this was the last time they
> would say goodbye to them ... In the same way as birds
> fly away when a storm blows up so we realised that we
> were going to have to flee when the Russians arrived.[23]

Marion von Dönhoff recounts how:

> The first who came were White Russian peasants with
> their horses and lightly loaded wagons on which most

of their small amount of possessions and the smallest children were sitting. The rest of the family walked beside the wagons whilst the farmers with their high fur hats walked in front to lead the horse.[24]

Although the rumours from the Baltic front were that the Red Army was almost at the East Prussian borders, government propaganda broadcast on the radio promised the people that the Eastern Front was strong from Tilsit to Kattowitz. Huge Nazi slogans were painted on town walls to encourage the German people to resist and they were told the Russians could be stopped. In the meantime they were assured that *Wunderwaffen* – 'wonder weapons' – were nearly ready. Final victory was on the horizon.

It was not made clear what these so-called wonder weapons were. Perhaps they were the V-1 flying bomb and V-2 rocket which were being turned out at the special production base carved out under the Harz Mountains at the Nordhausen concentration camp, where 30,000 inmates slaved underground. Both weapons were troubled by technical difficulties and production was slow to get going. In the end neither weapon had the payload or accuracy to be the answer to Germany's problems on the Eastern Front or elsewhere.

There is also some evidence that atomic experiments were going on at Nordhausen; German physicists had been at the forefront of atomic research just before the war broke out and continued to make slow progress, but Hitler was not impressed and the research went on in a desultory fashion and by 1945 Germany was a long way behind the USA in nuclear research.

The wonder weapons were fantasy and, if some East Prussian civilians were taken in by the propaganda, German soldiers on the front knew that defeat was imminent. They were retreating rapidly and, as they marched, Russian aircraft released leaflets exhorting them to surrender: 'German soldiers: you have been betrayed. Surrender to our units, which will rehabilitate you. You have lost the war!' In fact on the Baltic flank the Russian offensive was deliberately slow-moving and as yet limited in scale because the Red Army was concentrating its energies on the Belorussian front and Poland.

The first attacks on the city of Memel took place in August 1944 and refugees from there appeared in East Prussia. From east of the city, Labiau and Elchniederung were completely evacuated, and the refugees from their were joined by people from the other Baltic lands to the north, which the Russians had also entered. Streams of migrants with high-loaded horse-drawn *panje* wagons arrived asking for work on East Prussian farms. They spread out their goods and carts on the meadows outside villages and left their animals to graze. They came with terrible news of half-starved Russian troops, tired of fighting and of living, who brushed aside civilians without a qualm and slaughtered as they advanced; those who got away watched in mute horror. The Russians, when they were not fighting the German Army, pushed the tide of civilians along in front of them, firing at them and driving tanks through the terrified mobs. Even so, when news came that the Soviet Army had retreated, many Memellanders returned to their own farms to bring in the harvest, and ignored the warnings that the Russians would be back

A few weeks later, on Sunday 7 October, the people of Memel and villages near the town were once again given orders to pack their bags and get ready to leave. This time it was to be for good and everyone except police and the Volkssturm had to leave. Many made their way over to the Kurisches Nehrung. Here, ships and small boats were waiting to take them away. But other refugees, possibly a third of all those who fled from the Memel area, were caught by the Russians. Many were robbed, raped and then killed.

The people of the district of Heydekrug left it too late to get away. The few survivors remember how no warnings were given to them by the authorities. When Russian tanks entered on 9 October, daily life was completely normal. The trains were running, shops were open and housewives were queuing for their rations when the attack began. Farmers working outside in the surrounding fields were run down as they tried to flee and three trains on the nearby rail line were bombarded. Many of the local inhabitants were arrested and those considered fit for work were sent to Russia to toil in labour camps. After the Russian attack on the countryside around Memel, the area was left, in the words of a Russian soldier 'as still as death'. At Yalta in 1945 Stalin declared that no Germans would be left in East Prussia after the Russian invasion: 'Once our troops have marched through,' he predicted, 'the Germans will flee', but the policy had already been put into practice in the Memelland in 1944.

Guy Sajer arrived with his division on the coast south of Memel a few weeks later and found the area crowded with people. 'The town was still alive but in ruins beneath the flames, the smoke-darkened sky, the throb of Russian fighter-bombers, the heavy artillery, the terror and the whirling snow.' His unit was ordered to deal with the thousands of refugees trying to escape by sea. He saw horrific scenes, with women half crazed with hunger, cold and fear. Old people killed themselves and mothers seized guns from dead soldiers and shot themselves after handing over their children and their ration cards to other women. A few days later Sajer and his unit were sent to the outskirts of Memel where he witnessed the destruction of the once fine city by fire. It was an 'inferno, an apocalypse, an enormous catastrophe and a tomb'.[25]

The Russians overran the Baltic States in October 1944 and succeeded in isolating thirty divisions of Army Group North in Kurland, between the Gulf of Riga and the Baltic Sea. On 16 October the Soviet Army launched a massive attack against the German Fourth Army on the eastern frontier of East Prussia. They broke through the frontier three days later and captured the districts of Goldap and Gumbinnen.

On 21 October news broke that the Russians had attacked the village of Nemmersdorf. It was the first German village where a large number of civilians fell into Soviet hands. The troops were the 25th Tank Division and they rolled in from Gumbinnen. As they approached, the locals tried to flee but to do so they had to cross the only bridge across the River Angerapp. The Russian commanders gave the order full speed ahead and Russian tanks rolled over a whole crowd of refugees who were attempting to flee the village. Russian troops captured the bridge at 7.30 a.m., shooting escapees as they came. All the women were captured and raped and some were left crucified on the doors of houses and barns. Children were clubbed to death and old men were shot in cold blood. When the German Army retook the village two days later they claimed to have found nearly all the 653 inhabitants dead.[26] Soldier Günter Koschorrek later described in his diary finding an old man 'whose throat had been drilled through with a pitchfork so that his entire body is hanging on a barn door . . . It is impossible for me to describe all the terrible sights we have witnessed in Nemmersdorf.'[27]

It was the soldiers' first glimpse of what was to become a familiar sight in the next few months. Whereas, as time went on, the Nazis were keen to suppress such news, in October 1944 the events in Nemmersdorf were used by Goebbels for propaganda purposes to firm up resistance to the Russians. Nevertheless, the truth was that in Nemmersdorf it became clear that the perpetrators of the war were about to become its victims. 'The fighting,' as James Charles Roy so aptly puts it, 'was fearsome, a wintry replication of the horror of Stalingrad played out a hundredfold in city squares and village markets throughout East Prussia.'[28]

If the Nazi authorities had drawn the right conclusions from the events at Nemmersdorf they would immediately have set about making evacuation plans for the 2.5 million Germans who lived in East Prussia, the 1.9 million in East Pomerania and the 4.7 million in Silesia. But in Hitler's Reich such thoughts were forbidden and Hitler remained, at least publicly, convinced that the Third Reich would survive. The only evacuation permitted was from the eastern borders of the province, and even from these districts it usually came too late and without any forward planning so that the trains were over-full or left without all of the refugees, leaving many to the mercy of the Russians.

Otto Schneidereit's wife, children and parents were amongst those who left. Terrible sorrow overwhelmed the family as they prepared to leave the village where they had lived for ten years. They sat in their garden for one last time and ate the soft fruit which they had grown there. Then, as darkness fell, they left their home, whilst Otto returned to his unit near Tilsit where the battlefront was drawing closer.[29]

In Königsberg, Michael Wieck's employer, Herr Mendelsohn, took him to the top of the factory building. He had to concentrate very hard 'but then I hear it clearly. Like an endless thunderstorm it is rumbling and roaring without a pause,' for in the distance was the sound of battle still very far away but audible. The war had moved onto German soil:

> The contrast of the present situation to the previous arrogance and the victory slogans could not have been more stark. Confusion grew, doubt stalled action,

collapse was imminent and now only a few believed Goebbels's drivel about a wonder weapon that would win the war.[30]

That October Hans von Lehndorff, a doctor working in Königsberg, recalls that he could see at night the eastern borders of the province lit up like a rainbow of fire – the towns, cities and farms of Memel, Tilsit, Schirwindt, and Eydtkuhnen, all being bombed by the Russians. There were a couple of additional bombing raids on Königsberg and every day they knew the enemy was getting closer; the front was less than a hundred kilometres away. No one would speak about what was going on out there, only hope that no one had been left behind. For a couple of days there was an inestimable number of refugees on the road and then it was quiet – almost inexplicably quiet:

The roar from the front stopped, the firing stopped and the nightly flight of storks restarted. How bewitchingly the deserted land lay with its farms and villages in the brilliance of an incomparable autumn.[31]

The Russians had paused in their advance for a few weeks in order to regroup, to reorganise supplies and to build up new reserves of men and weapons. Fighting continued, however, in Kurland and on 20 November a Russian artillery barrage pounded German Army Group North; the Germans were successful in containing the Soviet onslaught but then the late autumn rains set in, turning the terrain into a vast swampy morass and here, too, the Russians temporarily withdrew.

For East Prussia it was the calm before the storm. Some allowed themselves to be lulled into a false sense of security, even though Königsberg was filling up with refugees from the East Prussian countryside and soldiers came marching in in open formation, as if ready for immediate battle, as an eyewitness recalled, exactly ten paces apart. They wore white to camouflage themselves from the winter landscape and had terrible tales to tell of what the Russians had done. Helga Gerhardi heard something from her mother that she found very alarming:

> Her face looked troubled and worried. 'I went to see Mrs Jacoby this morning and we had quite a talk. She is leaving Königsberg with her sister and going to stay with relatives.'

Helga's mother had heard other things from Mrs Jacoby:

> 'She said that they have pushed much farther into East Prussia than we are told on the radio. She is convinced that the Germans are going to lose the war ... We have already heard terrible stories about the animal behaviour of the Russians and the way they treat women. If the Russians should come to Königsberg, God forbid that this happens, you might think it would be better to be dead than to be desecrated by them. Mrs Jacoby has given me some poison. It is cyanide. It is a very quick killer. I have two phials.'[32]

In spite of the precarious situation, Erich Koch would still not allow any plans to be made for the complete evacuation of the area. Declaring that 'East Prussia will remain forever German', he announced that it was quite unnecessary to leave. Officials received strict instructions that they were to report any instances of preparation for flight. Posters declared 'Our Walls May Be Broken But Our Hearts Are Not'. The Mayor of Insterburg, about eighty kilometres from Königsberg, was horrified when he realised that the frontier would soon be overrun with enemy troops. Whilst Koch made plans to hold out till the last, the Insterburg mayor developed a detailed evacuation plan for his townsfolk – a plan which resulted in the majority of the inhabitants getting away when the attack on the town came early the following year. But the timely and organised clearing of Insterburg was not repeated elsewhere. It was left to individuals to make their own decisions as to whether or not to leave. Many now began to feel very uneasy; no one really knew how the war was going and the Nazi propaganda machine ran very efficiently. To doubt Germany's victory was treason and to voice doubts meant death to the unbeliever. 'Where was the Russian army?' Helga Gerhardi wanted to know, and 'How many German soldiers were there to fight them? Were we being told the truth, or was there a cover up?'[33]

Hans von Lehndorff recalls that things remained strangely still:

... until the November storms had cleared the land and the frost sparkled on the last grass in the meadows. Everywhere on the fields, on the roads and railway embankments we could see the herds of cows, which had now become wild, becoming weaker and weaker. As the first snows came, they faltered and one after another died. Christmas came and then fourteen days later it was all over.[34]

In Königsberg the number of wounded soldiers brought to hospitals had begun to increase sharply in the weeks before Christmas 1944. Coal was short and the wards were bitterly cold; there was an acute shortage of medical supplies and most of the bandages were paper. There was a first-aid post at the Hauptbahnhof where the wounded waited to be assessed. The station had been heavily bombed and most of its roof was missing. It was draughty, cold and full of ice and snow. Wounded soldiers were often just dumped on a train because there was no field hospital at the front; Königsberg was the first place where they could get medical attention. Many lay only on straw and a thin blanket in goods trucks. Some were already dead from their wounds or had been overwhelmed by the frost and extreme cold in the carriages. The temperature was often 20 degrees below zero. They told the nurses and doctors that the Russians were approaching and the frightening thing was that none of them had travelled very far. There was no official news about what was going on and the lack of information was almost unbearable. People became increasingly nervous.

By this time there was a severe fuel shortage in Königsberg, and wood burning gasifiers[35] powered the few trucks on the roads. Horse-drawn wagons were now the chief means of transport and heavy war equipment was seldom seen despite the growing threat of attack. Fear mounted among civilians as Russian planes flew unchallenged over the city both by day and night. Everyone who was fit enough was drafted to construct tank traps which, when they were eventually put to the test, proved to be totally ineffective. Outside the city the Volkssturm, under armed guard, continued to dig trenches and foxholes; crossroads were fortified. Sentries stood on every corner looking for deserters. The people of Königsberg waited in fear for the Russian assault.

Christmas 1944 was a strange time; Hans von Lehndorff recorded how, at his home near Insterburg:

> Christmas came and went and everyone in their own homes celebrated almost with joy as in the old days. Even hunts were organised and people met up to finish off the year in the traditional ways.[36]

Marion von Dönhoff also went hunting with her family that Christmas but, whilst they enjoyed their day in the fresh snow in the forests, she could not help thinking of how 'ten thousand German and Russian soldiers were bleeding to death' on that icy winter's day.[37] In Nordenburg, about a hundred kilometres from Königsberg, where his father was the pastor of the Protestant church, Werner Terpitz and his younger brothers and sisters had a 'proper Christmas celebration with walks in the snow and sledging and endless games'. They were all good musicians and, 'We formed a family choir but mine was the only male voice as father preferred to listen.' For the Terpitz family:

> The new year began normally; we had no idea that in a few short weeks 700 years of German history would come to an end. But we had a presentiment and things began to weigh us down [even though] there were people who even now spoke of victory, or of home-coming after flight. We thought they were foolish; of course everyone hoped for a miracle but we dared not speak of it or of our fears. The all-seeing dictator might have found out what we were thinking.[38]

In Kurland, Gottlob Bidermann remembers how:

> . . . the inevitable questions became more dominant in every conversation. What will become of this? How will it end? Is it to be an endless horror from which there will be no escape?[39]

And at her home near Berlin, Lali Horstmann faced the New Year with trepidation:

> Outwardly there was nothing sombre on the 1st of January 1945. The sky was brilliant blue and the sun gleamed on the snowflakes falling softly from the sky. The morning mail reminded us of the terrible general situation. A friend in East Prussia who lived in a

beautiful house, which had been in her family for generations, wrote how she feared the Russian advance and its consequences. A jar of honey from Silesia was accompanied by a brief note, 'the last I shall ever send you from home'.[40]

Yet even in the first days of January many people in Königsberg still seemed unaware of the true state of the war. No one was allowed to listen to any foreign news and the only information received was what Goebbels was prepared to tell them. His propaganda machine was very efficient and to doubt him was dangerous. Those who remember the last days before the onslaught on East Prussia recall that there were still many who believed the message from Berlin that there was nothing to fear. The propaganda given out day after day was that the German Army was holding the attackers back and that the Russians had been stopped. A few weeks later it became clear that all civilians should have been evacuated to the west when the trains were still running but the authorities did nothing; people went about their day-to-day business in their damaged city and tried to put their fears out of their minds.

Chapter Ten

'A VAST FLOOD OF HUMAN MISERY'

The Russian attack on East Prussia, which began on 12 January 1945, had been carefully planned but there was no indication from Hitler that he properly comprehended what was about to happen. He had installed himself as total master of the German war machine but he had not put in place any coherent plan to deal with the impending attack. General Guderian, the Army Chief of Staff responsible for the conduct of the war on the Eastern Front, had warned Hitler in October 1944 of what was likely to happen. Instead, in November Hitler transferred his attention and the available reserves away from the east to the Western Front and preparations for the ill-fated Ardennes Offensive against the American forces, an attack which began on 16 December leaving the Eastern Front very vulnerable.

In the New Year Guderian went to Hitler's headquarters at Ziegenberg in Hesse where the Führer had moved from the Wolf's Lair, 'to try to impress on Hitler the imminent danger posed by the Russians'. Guderian wearily explained that the Soviet Army on the Eastern Front was superior to the German forces in every respect. The Russians had eleven infantry soldiers for each German. They had seven tanks to each German one and their artillery outnumbered the Wehrmacht's by twenty-one to one. Hitler was dismissive. Stalin's army, he declared, was the 'greatest bluff since Genghis Khan' and it was to no avail that Guderian tried to tell him that 'the Eastern Front is like a house of cards; if the front is broken through at one point all the rest will collapse, for twelve and a half divisions are far too small a reserve for so extended a front.'[1]

In a show of ostrich politics Hitler's reply was that, 'The Eastern Front must help itself and make do with what it's got.' Completely unwilling to accept military advice from any general, he put Himmler in charge of much of the operations in the east. Himmler had little understanding of the problems facing the German forces and no idea how the situation might be resolved. He spoke as if the armies available to defend the eastern frontiers of Germany were at full strength in both men and equipment and seemed unaware that fighting in the autumn had weakened them. To keep men at their posts Himmler decided to make examples of those who opposed his plans. The police chief of Bromberg was shot for allegedly deserting and the mayor, who left without giving any orders, was hanged.

The Russian plan of campaign was for the Second Belorussian Front to make a thrust from the south and southwest to cut off East Prussia and then to proceed towards Berlin. At the same time the Third Belorussian Front would carry out an attack from the east along the River Pregel against Königsberg. The main assault would be launched with four field armies and two tank corps from around Gumbinnen in the direction of Wehlau.[2] The Red Army soldiers were relatively untrained but they had 'an exponential lead' over the Germans 'in weaponry, vehicles and aircraft'.[3] They enjoyed the element of surprise and above all they were on the offensive, determined to right the wrongs of nearly four years of bloody warfare against Germany.

Fired up by the memories of Nazi atrocities in the Soviet Union, and their fury made worse as they relieved concentration camps on their way west, the Russian soldiers hardly needed the added impetus of the propaganda of the Soviet writer Ilya Ehrenburg. He stirred up the troops to butcher all Germans who came their way with exhortations such as:

> The time has come to reckon with the Germans; crush forever the fascist beast in its den. Break the racial pride of the German woman. Take her as your legitimate booty.[4]

When they arrived at the German frontier they were faced by posters reminding them that it was their duty to wreak vengeance. Each day they were bombarded with patriotic and anti-Nazi propaganda. It was drummed into their heads that, 'Every metre of Prussia is drowned in the blood of the Slavic people.' Every detachment had a political officer whose duties were not only to indoctrinate the rank and file, but also to watch for and report any sign of disobedience, pacifism, defeatist mood or anti-Soviet activity.

The Third Belorussian Front was under the command of General Chernyakhovsky. His plan was to attack the German forces holding the Tilsit–Insterburg line to the east of Königsberg and then to seize the villages of Nemonien, Darkehmen and Goldap. After this Soviet troops would move west along the south bank of the River Pregel in the direction of Königsberg. Originally it was planned that the attacks would start on 20 January but on 6 January Winston Churchill asked Stalin whether the attack in the east could be brought forward in order to reduce pressure on the US and British forces slogging it out against the Germans in the Ardennes. Stalin agreed readily and, although weather conditions were not good, the rescheduling of the attack took German forces by surprise. General Georg-Hans Reinhardt was in charge of defending East Prussia but Hitler gave him little freedom to make decisions. He had three armies at his disposal: the Third Panzer Army guarding the northern and eastern access to Königsberg, the Fourth Army holding a salient in Masuria on the western edge of the province and the Second Army in the south of East Prussia.

On 12 January 1945 when the new campaign began, ten Russian armies crossed the River Vistula into Poland and launched a ferocious attack on the Germans. They made a clean breakthrough and overwhelmed whole formations; those which managed to survive were split into disorganised fragments. Realising at last the seriousness of what was happening, Hitler left Ziegenberg and returned to his bunker in Berlin from where he ordered two Panzer divisions away from East Prussia to defend Kielce way to the south of Warsaw but it was too late – Poland had been liberated. Facing a mighty Russian force, a depleted German Army was left under orders to hold on to the bitter end and to try to counter-attack and to regain territory which was lost.

On 13 January the Third Belorussian Front opened its offensive against East Prussia between Gumbinnen and Schlossberg. It was a foggy winter morning, with a light covering of frost and snow. The people had received no warning and now in the villages there was panic.[5] Although German commanders had previously asked permission to evacuate civilians, Hitler had rejected their requests as defeatist and ordered his Gauleiters to keep them in their homes. As a result the East Prussian civilians were to bear the brunt of Russian reprisals. The attack on East Prussia was savage; with revenge for all that had been suffered in German hands in the forefront of their minds, the Russian advance was characterised by arson, plunder and rape. The most terrible vengeance was taken on any home which showed signs that the occupants had been Nazis. German officials, who had proudly worn their uniforms when the Russians arrived, lay strewn in the street with bullets in their heads.

People began to pack up and leave in haste; women, children and the elderly – the few men who had avoided call-up because of their age or state of health were now mostly fighting with the Volkssturm – all strove to get away from the Russian advance. It was the coldest winter on record and in temperatures of –20 Celsius columns of refugees made their way towards Königsberg and the coast through snowy days and freezing nights. The refugees, mingling with groups of Allied prisoners of war and freed slave labourers, trudged on foot or rode on farm carts through the bitter weather. Fathers sometimes shot all their families or gave them poison rather than face any more horror.

Hannelore Thiele was thirteen when her family had to pack up and leave. Her worst memory was of seeing her grandfather cry as he kept repeating that he would never see his home again. She recalled: 'That's what we all knew in our hearts, that we would never be coming back.'[6]

For Hannelore it was a farewell to both her home and childhood:

> What a way to leave! The stalls were full of livestock. The cows were untied, the pig pens opened, chicken and geese were scattered . . . everything had to be left behind. It was bitterly cold. We had all put on as much clothing as possible for the snow was frozen hard and the streets had turned to ice. The roads were clogged with refugees and again and again low-flying aircraft passed over, shooting at us.[7]

As Red Army soldiers moved westwards they took unprepared villages and farms by surprise, and ransacked them. They raped women and girls, and shot or hanged elderly men. They opened fire on trains carrying civilians to safety, slaughtered columns of refugees, crushed people and animals with their tanks and machined-gunned anyone hiding in woods and ditches. Some were charged or crushed into a bloody smear of human and horse-flesh by the Soviet juggernaut. Raped women were nailed by their hands to farm carts carrying their families. Sometimes whole families were mown down.

The rage of the Soviet soldiers was terrible. There were very few who had not suffered in some way from the Nazi invasion. Most had lost relatives in the war and many had lost their homes and all their belongings under German occupation. The anti-Nazi propaganda of the Soviet Army was so strong that almost every soldier was overwhelmed by an insatiable craving for revenge. The first Germans they met suffered most. Many civilians were indiscriminately killed, women were raped, property was destroyed and German military warehouses plundered. Alcohol was available in abundance and Soviet soldiers got so drunk that they were sometimes hardly able to perform their duties. Senior officers tried to keep the rank and file under control, but it was an impossible task. The officers themselves were affected by a mixture of different emotions, including those of exhilaration, hatred and their sense of duty.[8]

Chernyakhovsky unleashed his main attack on Pilkallen, a few kilometres from Gumbinnen, on 16 January. Despite the terrible weather, the Third Panzer Army held the Russians off for a few days until 20 January when the Russians broke through the German defences and approached Tilsit, where the Volksgrenadiers and Volkssturm simply ran away. The civilian population was left to fend for itself. Those who escaped with their lives were thrown out of their homes and their animals were killed for meat or driven in herds to the Russian frontier.

In many villages the Russians marked out a centre point where loot was collected together. They stripped houses completely – the floors, doors, windows, washbasins, toilets, lamps, wires, switches – to be loaded onto Russian lorries later with shovels. They stole clothes, dressing themselves in anything from women's nightgowns to dinner jackets, and, fuelled by any alcohol they came by, they then burnt down the houses and barns even to the extent of depriving themselves of shelter.

The Russians captured 'Erwin Germanovitch' (as the historian Godfrey Lias called him) after Stalingrad. He spoke Ukrainian and after managing to escape from a labour camp contrived to join the Russian Army. He was in charge of a Red Army unit which marched into Germany early in 1945. He realised that the majority of the soldiers had never seen a decent house, decent furniture or a well-dressed woman until they reached Germany. One day he even found some soldiers washing their hands in a toilet bowl:

> They had not the slightest idea how to use a water closet or where to put the paper when they had done so. Furniture, including beds, was to the ordinary Russian soldiers, something which took up space which was better occupied by human bodies. Sometimes they burnt it, sometimes they threw it out of the window and sometimes they carried it out and dumped it out in the garden.

He remembered, too, that:

> . . . during the advance the Russian army raped, looted, and drank everything it found in a bottle even

if the bottle had a death's head on it and it was labelled 'poison'. Many Russians died as a result.

Some of the Soviet soldiers were overwhelmed by what they had seen. Germanovitch caught sight of a letter a Russian had written home:

> I am in a good mood because I have seen so much in my short time in Germany – more than in my whole life. They know how to build in Germany. Imagine, in every village the houses and even the stables are of stone and brick and there is electric light everywhere. When I first went into such a house there was so much furniture I could scarcely get through it and, imagine, such a flat is only for one family, and it does not have only one room, but three or four and a bath, too, and a water toilet.[9]

On 21 January the Russian advance reached Tannenberg and the memorial to the German victory against the Russians in August 1914; now they razed it to the ground. The 21st was also a terrible day for the inhabitants of Wehlau. For two days the small town had been overwhelmed with refugees from farther north-east pushing their way down the single main street, Reichsstrasse 1, which was the main road from Insterburg to Königsberg. The German Army was trying to clear it to allow troops to get through and the refugees had been forced to camp in the horse market.

At 10.00 a.m. on 21 January the church bells of Wehlau were rung, signalling that all the inhabitants were to leave. Only officials were to remain behind. A couple of trains came through the station on the way to Königsberg but for most there was no room. The town began to resemble an ant's nest. The streets were completely blocked and the bridges were impassable. There was no time to say goodbye properly to a place which had been East Prussian for 700 years. All they could do was pack a few things and try to get out. Some were lucky and got a lift with the Army but most had to load their belongings on to carts or sledges and struggle through the crowded roads to get to Königsberg or to Samland, where they hoped to find a boat to take them west along the Baltic coast. The route was so crowded that for many it took twenty hours to go the fifteen kilometres to the safety of the next town, Allenburg. Some tried other routes out of the town to avoid Reichstrasse 1 but on these the refugees were caught by Russian artillery fire and many were killed. Those trying to get to Königsberg were attacked from the air and dead people, animals and broken carts littered the icy roads. Many committed suicide when they ran out of energy.[10]

Such late instructions to pack up and go were typical. Gauleiter Koch had decreed that only people who lived in the east of the province and were under immediate threat should be told to leave. The rest were told that there was no danger and that they should stay where they were. The result was that instructions to leave came at the last minute and, as there had been no planning, the consequence was panic. Trains were packed or did not come at all, and the weather was so bad that many East Prussians convinced themselves that to fall into the hands of the Russians could not be as bad as they imagined and they simply decided to stay.

They could not have been more wrong. In one village taken over by the Russians an eyewitness saw how:

> The vehicles had rolled over people, flattening them in the ice and snow. The houses had broken windows and doors and in the streets were broken china and household goods. The buildings had been completely smashed, houses and barns were half burnt out and some were only a heap of rubble and ash. That was the

extent of the material damage. It was what had happened to the people that made us scream and made even the hardest of us retch and be sick and be absolutely petrified. Women had had their clothes slit open. Some were naked. They had been raped and lay on bare floors, or in the street, frozen stiff or dead. There were young girls no more than fifteen or sixteen years old. There were old women; age didn't seem to matter. An old man was nailed upside down on the door of the shed. Along the wall of a house was a row of bodies, all old men and young boys, shot in the back.[11]

To avoid rape, young women tried to disguise themselves in old women's clothes but once they had heard the words 'Frau, komm' uttered in a thick Russian accent they knew there was no escape. Sometimes the attacker would come on his own but frequently a whole armed gang would each take their turn. A woman diarist remembered the horror of an attack by a lone Russian soldier:

Shut your eyes, clench your teeth, and don't utter a sound. Only when the underwear is ripped apart with a tearing sound, the teeth grind involuntarily . . . I feel the fingers at my mouth, smell the reek of horses and tobacco . . . Then the man above me slowly lets his spittle dribble into my mouth.[12]

The congestion on all the escape routes was unbelievable, especially at river crossings. Sometimes refugees would be overtaken not by the Russians but by the retreating German troops. Their heavy equipment would simply crush any civilians who got in the way. Soldiers were under orders not to give any help to those fleeing the Russians; they simply passed by the broken-down carts, those wounded by Russian air attacks and the elderly and the very young who did not have the stamina to endure the freezing conditions. Marion von Dönhoff had been planning her flight for months. Her saddlebag and rucksack were packed with a few necessities. She left the village of Quittainen on horseback with fellow villagers on 24 January, when an order came just forty-eight hours after they had been told to stay at home. She and her maid, her cook and her secretary ate one last evening meal together and then at midnight set out on their journey, leaving the remains of their supper on the table and the doors unlocked. There was, she remembers, no time for a proper farewell even though she realised that she would never return. Outside the temperature was –20 Celsius, the snowdrifts were a metre deep and the roads were icy. When the trek reached Preussisches Holland, the next town, just eleven kilometres away, after a gruelling sixteen-hour journey, she rode ahead to the Nazi Party headquarters to ask where they should head for next. She found the building deserted, the windows and doors open and papers and orders blowing around in the cold wind. Everyone had gone – the brownshirts had abandoned the people and saved their own skins. Some of her companions thought it might be best to return home. Marion warned them that the Russians would kill them but many thought she was wrong. 'We can work for them and plough the fields and milk the cows,' they said and did not seem to understand that they would be shot or taken away to labour camps in the Soviet Union.[13]

Those who could made for Pillau where numerous ships were waiting to evacuate the refugees to the west. They came in their thousands from Königsberg, Cranz, Heiligenbeil, Elbing and Preussisches Holland, 'a vast flood of human misery slowly washing toward the safety that had been promised'. Near the quayside there was a large metal cross which stood on a slight elevation, glittering with frost. Some of the crowd collected there each day to listen to prayers and the words of a pastor.[14]

Pregnant women had priority on the departing ships, then children and the elderly. Fit and healthy civilian men, though there were few of them, had little chance of being taken for they were to stay to participate in the final defence of the province. Wounded soldiers were also eligible for embarkation – all except the most severely injured whose chances of survival were doubtful or those who were severely mutilated. For them everything was over. Even by the harbourside the bombardments never ceased and there was almost constant panic among the waiting crowds. These crowds stretched as far as the eye could see trapped on the quayside in front of a large port building which was also crammed with people. Guy Sajer remembers the sound of their thudding feet, like a dull roll of muffled guns, as people stamped to keep themselves warm, and he recalls the solitary children who had lost their mothers whose tears instantly froze as they ran down their cheeks.[15]

Around 450,000 people left Pillau between January and April 1945 in the hope of finding freedom, even though the road route to the port from Königsberg was blocked by the Russians between 26 January and 20 February when the German Army managed to reopen it. Admiral Konrad Engelhardt was in charge of the naval operation to evacuate East Prussia in these last four months of the war, under orders of Grand Admiral Karl Dönitz. Dönitz said that:

> The salvation of the German eastern population [was] the one essential task which our armed services still had to perform. If, to our sorrow, we could not protect the homes of our eastern fellow countrymen . . . the least we could do was to ensure that they escaped with their bare lives.

Yet more pragmatically, as he admits in his memoirs:

> This was not the only reason. The Allies were
> unshakeable in their determination that there would
> be no end to the war other than by unconditional
> surrender. For the German armed forces this meant
> that all the movement of troops would cease the
> moment that the capitulation was signed. Had we
> capitulated during the winter months of 1944–5 three
> and a half million soldiers on the Eastern Front would
> have fallen into the hands of the Russians.

Dönitz was well aware of what the consequences would be. To save as many civilians and military personnel as possible he organised a fleet of over a thousand ships (672 merchant ships and 409 naval vessels) to evacuate hundreds of thousands of people from the ports of Königsberg, Pillau, Danzig, Neufahrwasser and Gotenhafen.[16] It is estimated that around 2.5 million civilians and soldiers were evacuated in this period in a naval operation which was efficient and carried out with considerable courage.

On 21 January Hans von Lehndorff crossed the large square in front of the Hauptbahnhof and found it overflowing with refugees. There were rows and rows of laden carts and there was a constant flow of newcomers, mainly women. Trains were returning to the station as it was no longer possible to get through to the west and most of the passengers were now determined to escape via Pillau. One woman took him aside to say that she was not worried. 'The Führer won't let us fall into Russian hands,' she said and Lehndorff privately wondered why she still had so much trust.[17]

On 22 January the Russians reached Insterburg.[18] On 23 January the Russian Fifth Guards Tank Army reached Elbing near the southern end of the Frisches Haff and reached the Haff itself on 24 January. East Prussia was now severed from the rest of the Reich and eight divisions of the Second Army were cut off in the province together with all the Fourth Army and the remains of the Third Panzer Army. In the villages around Elbing the message came on the night of 21/22 January that the people should pack up and leave. All the roads were jammed with people trying to flee but now the Russians moved east to Braunsberg and delivered a blow which trapped the German Army in the Heiligenbeil *Kessel* (cauldron) to the south of the Frisches Haff.

In Königsberg everyone's nerves were increasingly on edge for no one knew what was going to happen. The official orders were still that, 'East Prussia will be held; an evacuation is out of the question', and most people now passively accepted the fact that up to this point there had been no orders and no preparations for evacuating civilians. 'We had the impression they would press weapons into our hands so we could fight to prolong the lives of those who had brought all this about in the first place,' wrote Michael Wieck. He recalls how the 'tongue telegraph was working at full speed and not a day went by without more rumours and unbelievable stories of the atrocities of the Russian soldiers.'[19]

The way out to the west was now completely blocked and the only means of escape from Königsberg was over the frozen Frisches Haff to the Nehrung and from there to Gotenhafen and Danzig where ships were waiting. The weather was brutal. Each day that January icy winds swept across the countryside which was covered by deep snow. Thousands crowded on to the frozen Haff to cross the ice and with their silhouettes standing out against the ice they were an easy target for Russian attack. Many died from cold and exhaustion, particularly the very old and the young. Their bodies had to be abandoned along the way, although many mothers continued to cuddle their dead babies against their breasts in the vain hope of reviving them. Sometimes the ice was not thick enough to bear the weight and horses and people drowned. Refugees used this route for several weeks until the end of February when the ice began to thaw. Guy Sajer's unit had been ordered to withdraw from Pillau and the men were making their way along the Frisches Nehrung with the thousands of civilians. He watched them tramping along the frozen tracks and feared for the children who 'stared about them with unseeing eyes' and were 'being punished before they had committed any crime'.[20]

Helga Gerhardi was one who fled from Königsberg at this time. She remembers packing a few possessions, and then leaving the house tidy for she was convinced that she would come back: 'Surely the German Army would be able to push the Russians back. I did not know that I would never return.' Helga went first to the Hauptbahnhof where she discovered trains were still leaving but only for people with permits: 'The SS stood at the barriers with guns, preventing the mass of people from pushing through and getting to the trains.' Only Party members could travel. Crowds of people were waiting in the icy, roofless station and there was no food or drink and no toilets.

Realising that there was no alternative, she decided to go to the Pregel harbour in the town centre and try to get on a boat travelling along the sea canal across the Haff to Pillau where she might get a ship to the west. There were many small boats there, including coal boats which travelled in front and acted as ice-breakers. There were hundreds of other people there too, some of whom had been waiting for days. There was no organisation and no guidance, and when she got there no one was selling tickets for the waiting ships. The captains of the coal boats were using people's desperation to make money by demanding large sums to transport them. They took jewellery, money and other valuables and some desperate families gave them all they had.

It was much too cold to stay for days at the harbour waiting for a kind captain who would take me at a reasonable price. If I walked to Pillau I would again be confronted with having to fork out a huge sum of money to get on a boat. I decided to go with the people who wanted to go along the edge of the Haff towards the west and then make my way to Elbing.[21]

On the Haff were many other refugees who recall finding their way along unsignposted icy roads with abandoned carts and belongings littering the way and dead bodies in the ditches. The roads were jammed with the columns of refugees, driving their herds of cattle and horses. Above them circled Russian night-fighters which shot at the slowly moving columns of refugees with machine guns.[22]

When the refugees reached the southern banks of the Haff at Heiligenbeil they were stopped by German troops who told them that, with the Russians holding Elbing, the only means of escape was across the frozen Haff to the Nehrung and then on to Danzig or Gotenhafen and then to try to get a boat to the west. The Haff was covered by columns of carts, wagons and animals, moving painfully slowly along a road staked out to provide a safe route across where the ice was thickest. The road had been made by military engineers with the help of fishermen. Wooden boards lined the route and the people were told to keep fifteen metres' distance between the wagons otherwise the ice might break. On either side of the marked route were abandoned carts and horses and human bodies. People had thrown all but the bare necessities from their wagons to make them lighter.

Refugees hoped that when they eventually left the ice and reached the snow-covered Nehrung it would be easier to reach safety but they found that to prevent the Russians from moving along the narrow land strip of the Nehrung soldiers had built barriers from wood and rubbish – but these also prevented the refugees from progressing and they had to struggle on to the sandy Baltic beaches to continue their journeys. On the Nehrung there was no bread and no fresh water and nothing to give to the animals.

Further west, Marianne Mackinnon made her escape overland:

> For hours we walked in a herd, measuring time in degrees of hunger, frostbite and exhaustion, and by the gradual dissolution of daylight. Colonies of crows mottled the wintry fields, in which wretches scraped the ground in the hope of finding an unharvested potato, a beet or anything edible. A buzzard kept circling over some dark object, its ghoulish cries sounding like a prophecy of doom. It was difficult to know what was more unnerving – the deep rumbling front approaching from the east or the shuffling and dragging of hundreds of feet over the snow-crusted surface of the road. Night came early – a white and beautiful night, infinitely cold and cruel, in which a full moon dwelled lovingly on the chilling poetry of the naked fields ... And now more people dropped out, collapsing quietly by the road or choosing the deceptive shelter of ditches or hedges for a place to rest, perhaps not realising, perhaps not caring, that they might drift into a sleep from which there was no waking.[23]

Gauleiter Erich Koch had never intended to stand by those he had condemned to face the Russian attack. His personal possessions were already in western Germany and he abandoned Königsberg on 22 January, moving to a hotel near the port of Pillau from where he issued orders about how the defence of the city was to be conducted. Having steadfastly refused to allow anyone to leave when it was safe to do so, Koch now sent orders that the people should flee after all, once the Russians had broken in. Whilst he had escape transport arranged (a small plane, a ship and two ice-breakers were ready waiting for him) the population would have to escape by way of the road around the north side of the Pregel to Pillau where they would be subject to the constant danger of Russian artillery attack. When Koch finally fled by boat a few weeks later, he ordered the crew to bar the ship to any other refugees, leaving them on the quayside desperately begging to be allowed to sail with him to safety.

On 26 January thousands of refugees waiting on the quayside at Pillau were killed when the ammunition depot was blown up. Then, just a few days later, on 30 January 1945, the largest passenger shipping disaster in history – far worse than the *Titanic* – occurred outside the port of Gotenhafen. Gotenhafen was a collection point for both civilians and wounded soldiers and thousands were awaiting transport on the quayside. One of the ships available to transport them was the *Wilhelm Gustloff*. The Nazis had built the *Wilhelm Gustloff* in the 1930s as a cruise liner, but when war broke out it was used as a hospital ship, ferrying casualties across the Baltic. On that night 60,000 people were waiting to escape from Gotenhafen and, as soon as the gangplanks were put in place, the desperate escapees tried to push their way on board. In the event 1,100 crew, 730 wounded soldiers, 373 young women who belonged to the Women's Naval Auxiliary and more than 6,000 civilian refugees, mostly women and young children, were packed into the ship – a total of over 9,000 people. Every last centimetre of space was taken. The temperature outside was −10 Celsius, it was snowing and the deck was covered with layers of ice. The ship was unescorted and, because the visibility was poor, the captain decided to sail out into the open sea rather than keep to coastal waters. At 9.10 p.m. a Russian submarine, which was off course because the captain had disobeyed orders, spotted the *Gustloff*. Four torpedoes were fired and three direct hits were made below the waterline. The thousands on board began to panic, with everyone pushing to get up on deck. They clawed their way upwards; children slipped from their mothers' arms and were crushed. The ship was sinking fast and many of the lifeboats were under water before they could be launched. Others were covered with such a thick layer of ice that they were too heavy to launch. It soon became obvious that the majority on board were doomed. The ship sank just fifty minutes after being hit and the water was so cold that no one could survive for more than a few minutes. Of the 9,000 people on board only 996 survived.[24]

The *Gustloff* was another tragedy amongst the thousands of others that occurred in Hitler's War and few beyond the victims' families mourned its sinking. As one of the few survivors said:

> The *Wilhelm Gustloff*, a mass grave bearing the names of thousands of people, has to warn us, the living, and influence the leaders of the world in such a way that wars, which bring unspeakable suffering to mankind, will never be allowed to start again.[25]

Towards the middle of February a thaw set in on the Haff and the ports became even harder to reach. Nevertheless, with the Russians closing in behind them, many still tried to make it across the rapidly thinning ice.

The destination that many hoped to reach was Berlin, but the authorities there could not cope. There was an ever-rising tide of refugees and wounded soldiers, and there was nowhere to house them and little to feed them. The city's coal reserves were down to a few weeks' supply, and rations, which by the end of February were down to 1,600 calories a day, could not be guaranteed to the new arrivals. Mingling with the fleeing East Prussians were prisoners of war, released by the German authorities as the Russians closed in. When Sybil Bannister arrived in Berlin by train in January 1945 after fleeing the Russians she was startled to find that Berliners seemed to have little idea of what was going on. Apart from the railwaymen, nobody in Berlin had heard that the German defences in the east had collapsed. There had been reports and rumours of the Russian attack but the people still suffered from the delusion that the frontiers of the Reich would be held at all costs. As far as they knew the trains arriving hour by hour in the city might have been bringing prisoners and not refugees. When the refugees were dealt with, they were treated with contempt and were regarded as scaremongers who, by evacuating the border towns 'unnecessarily', were lowering the morale of good citizens and the armed forces. They would learn soon enough, thought Sybil, when the Russians were on their doorsteps and the tanks began rolling through their streets.[26]

Meanwhile, there was no let-up in the sufferings of the Jews in East Prussia. As Soviet forces pushed towards the sea, the labour camps in the Danzig and Königsberg regions were evacuated, many by sea. More than 5,000 Jews were driven from these camps towards Palmnicken, a small fishing village beyond Königsberg, on the shores of the Baltic. During the march to the sea more than 700 were shot. There was no food and nothing to drink, and most did not survive the march; when they got to Palmnicken those who were still alive were put in a deserted factory and were given no food. When they left, apparently to be taken to the port, most were in fact shot. A member of the Hitler Youth in Palmnicken, Martin Bergau, was ordered to take part in this 'special assignment'. His group was told by the SS to go with the Volkssturm and escort some Jewish women. The column was taken to a quarry near the sea and the women were told to kneel down by a trench full of bodies. Then they were each shot with a bullet in the neck. Martin was in his early teens when he witnessed this:

> I went home, feeling ashamed and wretched. I could hear the rumbling from the front. What will become of us now? Obviously when the Russians get here we will have to defend ourselves to the bitter end. But they'll kill us because we are all guilty.[27]

The camp at Stutthof, on the Frisches Haff, which had been the first concentration camp established outside Germany in 1939, was amongst the last to be liberated by the Russians and up to the last the minute the exterminations went on. The camp was about forty kilometres east of Danzig in a wooded clearing at the mouth of the River Vistula. Once Stutthof had been a pleasant seaside resort for the people of Danzig but in 1939, on the edge of the little town, the area was put to a more sinister use. The camp was originally set up as an emergency internment centre for Polish dissidents but it was considerably enlarged in 1943 and embraced several satellite camps spread across a large part of East and West Prussia.[28] The inmates had been employed in workshops and factories turning out equipment and clothing for the German armed forces. Until 1944 there had been relatively few Jewish internees, but in June 1944 many were transferred to Stutthof from Auschwitz and from then until October between 20,000 and 30,000 Jewish women, originally from Hungary, arrived there. They were joined by thousands of other Jewish women and children who were transferred from Latvia, Lithuania and Estonia as the Soviet Army advanced into the Baltic States. By late autumn 1944 seventy per cent of the camp inmates were Jewish; the rest were Russians and Poles. The camp became so overcrowded that there were outbreaks of typhus and other highly infectious diseases.

On 25 January 1945, with Soviet forces only a few kilometres away, the camp commandant ordered a general evacuation of captives to the interior of the Reich, but there were far too many inmates to get away before the Russians began a bombardment. The final evacuation took place on 27 April. Many were marched by the SS to the Frisches Haff and were amongst those shot at Palmnicken. Those who remained to be liberated by the Russians were simply set free and left to fend for themselves. N. K. Shneidmann, a young Lithuanian jew recruited into the Red Army, was riding in a Soviet jeep near Danzig when he saw some of the Jewish women liberated by the Russians from Stutthof. They were:

> ... poorly dressed, exhausted from hard labour and malnutrition. I looked into their faces from a distance. All looked alike. There was the same mark of suffering and humiliation in all of them.[29]

In Königsberg things were grim. Young Werner Terpitz was at school in Königsberg when the city came under siege on 14 January 1945.[30] On the night of 19 January sixteen-year-old Werner received a written order. Like other boys of his age he was to start building tank traps. The Nazi authorities had had months to prepare but they had become victims of their own propaganda. It had always been claimed that there was no risk to Königsberg and now it was too late. The next morning, at 6.00 a.m., Werner went to the North Station and with other boys was sent out to the suburb of Quedenau where they were given shovels, wheelbarrows and other tools and had to dig with their unpracticed hands until they had blisters. They returned the next day to be told there was nothing to do and he believed that 'in this way the great plan came to nothing'. On the same day Terpitz heard that his family in Nordenburg were in grave danger. The Russians were coming much faster than expected and had already reached the River Deime in the north and were also approaching from the south; the people had been advised to leave. But there was an unwritten rule that the priest and his family should stay until the end. For fifteen years, since first coming to his parish, his father, Paul Terpitz, had kept a guest book and now he wrote the final entry.

> On 19 January 1945 the clearance of Nordenburg was ordered. The clearance is about to begin and we have to leave our house where we have always offered hospitality. The Lord sends us on our way to an uncertain future. He guards our Fatherland with his mercy. Hebrews 13:14.[31]

And underneath he wrote the family names 'Paul, Elisabeth, Georg, Wolfgang, and Aunt Brigitte'.

The following night Paul Terpitz said his last prayers in the unheated church with twenty parishioners and they sang a final farewell hymn to the church and town. The family drank the last of the champagne hidden away in the cellar and Werner's younger brother, Wolfgang, went to buy supplies. Well aware that the town would soon be empty, the dairy was giving away milk and real cream: 'Everyone could buy anything without ration cards and the bread was free.' The family went to the station on several occasions to try to escape but it was not until 10.00 a.m. on Tuesday 23 January that the final order to leave came. Everyone had to hurry to the station to get on a train in half an hour. When they got there they squeezed into the cattle trucks of the so-called rescue train and waited for four icy hours whilst news arrived that the Russians were only a few kilometres away. Then, in the last sunshine of the day, railway officials emptied the water tower ('Everything must be left in order') and the train moved away. The family stood all that night, wedged tightly against the other passengers. There was nowhere to sit, no shelter and no toilets; the train travelled by a circuitous route to avoid the Russians, taking nearly eighteen hours to travel the hundred kilometres to Königsberg. When they got there the family somehow became separated. Whilst Paul and his two sons got as far as Pillau, where his parishioners urged them to get on one of the ships which was about to leave, his wife had got off the train in Königsberg and found her way to her parents' house in Admiral Scheer Strasse in the Amalienlau suburb. The family was reunited on 25 January, grandparents, their disabled son, the five from Nordenburg and Werner.[32]

On the 31st Werner was called to have a medical inspection prior to possible recruitment into the Army or the Volkssturm. He was directed to a command post near the North Station where he joined a long queue. When his turn came he was told to undress and was pummelled and pinched by an army doctor, his sight and hearing were tested and he was declared fit for military service:

> We were stark naked for the whole examination. Naked boys and naked grandfathers. With us, the sixteen-year-olds and a couple of disabled middle-aged men, there were very many old men, mostly unfit for the purpose. One was very fat and had bad asthma; yet most were taken on, though we could hardly believe that they were fit enough to fight.[33]

By 26 January the Soviet Army had reached the outer defences of Königsberg and two days later the city was within a hair's breadth of falling into the hands of the Russians. But then the Soviets came to a halt, diverting their forces temporarily to Heiligenbeil where the German Fourth Army was cut off. Königsberg had a breathing space.

Chapter Eleven

FORTRESS KÖNIGSBERG

At the end of January 1945 Königsberg was packed with 300,000 refugees who had fled to the city hoping it would be the first stop on their flight to freedom. Unable to get any farther, they parked their prams, sledges and carts along the roadsides, crowded into the bombed and damaged buildings and released the horses which had drawn their carts since they left their villages. Many of these animals died of starvation and others were shot; Werner Terpitz recalls how the once beautiful streets were strewn with the carcasses of dead horses from which all edible meat had been taken. The streets in the town centre were full of rubble made into amateurish roadblocks and broken-down trams were abandoned where they had come to a stop. All the city's schools were shut on 23 January and the University closed its doors on 28 January.

By 26 January the whole of East Prussia was in Russian hands apart from a strip of land sixty kilometres in length and varying in width, which extended from the southern shores of the Frisches Haff to Königsberg.[1] With Elbing already captured, the encirclement of East Prussia was complete; on

27 January Königsberg was completely entrapped by a semicircle of Russian troops occupying both sides of the Pregel estuary.

On 28 January, on his thirty-third birthday, Otto Schneidereit was with his Army division in Metgehen, a garden suburb of Königsberg, which lay on the main route between the city and Pillau. The soldiers had been guarding the little town for two weeks because its pleasant surroundings had been covered with munitions factories and depots which churned out armaments for the German war effort. Now, on 28 January, the order came to evacuate because the Russians had arrived. They were to go to Königsberg to help defend the city.

The next day, on 29 January, the Russians dealt what could have been a mortal blow when they overran Metgehen and then thrust towards the Haff to the west, completely blocking the way to Pillau. This marked the beginning of the first siege of Königsberg. Despite the blockade a train left the town for Pillau that morning. The track was blocked by a Russian tank, and the passengers were pulled out and subjected to a violent attack by Red Army soldiers.

With Königsberg isolated, Russian planes flew low and unchallenged over the city. If the gunners saw someone move they fired on them, and if they saw a vehicle they bombed it. People began to fear clear mornings because bright blue skies meant the fighters would be lurking. Life in Königsberg became extremely unpleasant. The weather continued to be exceptionally cold, with night-time temperatures as low as −28 degrees Celsius and fuel in short supply. The city was under constant artillery fire. Families had to find what shelter they could underground.

On 30 January, the twelfth anniversary of his coming to power, Hitler broadcast to the German nation for the last time. He called on each one of his people, 'To do his duty to the last and be willing to take upon himself every sacrifice he will be asked to make, with complete disregard for his personal safety.' He did not mention the military disasters of the previous weeks. Of the 'horrible fate now taking place in the east and eradicating people in their tens of thousands in villages, in the marches, in the country and in the towns', his only comment was that the Russians would be 'fought off and mastered'.[2]

For the next ten weeks the Russians encircled the city. The outer forts around the city, which had been built at the end of the nineteenth century, remained in German hands, but beyond this ring the Soviet Army entrenched, waiting to pounce. It was a strange time; Germany effectively ended at the rubble wall so hastily built by the volunteers; around it telegraph wires blew about in the wind and from behind came the constant rattle of artillery fire and Russian loudspeakers blaring out propaganda.

There was still water and electricity, and some food supplies for the civilians, refugees and the soldiers bombed out of their units who were trapped in the city. The SS were out looking for men capable of fighting. Many soldiers, who had taken refuge in Königsberg after fleeing from the front, imagined that the Russians would soon break in and had donned civilian clothes and tried to hide from the SS. Terpitz recalls how some were dragged out of their hiding places and were hanged as a deterrent to others:

> In front of the North Station the corpses lay in the snow day after day with staring eyes. They wore badges which read 'We were cowards and died as a result.'[3]

General Otto Lasch, appointed 'Fortress Commander of Königsberg' on 5 February, attempted to restore order. The city was full of refugees and he tried to find accommodation for them whilst making use of troops who had taken refuge in the city by forming them into fighting units. In the city huge yellow placards went up: 'All sixteen-year-olds have until 3 February to register with the Volkssturm or the Army.' The penalty for failing to do this was death. The notices appeared over General Lasch's signature.

Königsberg was one of several towns in the east designated a fortress – *Festung* – and now Hitler ordered that it must not surrender. Lasch set up his headquarters in an air-raid shelter in the Paradeplatz and from there he attempted to organise the defence of the city. He was short of troops, having at his disposal only four burnt-out divisions including one made up of under-trained Volksgrenadiers. He marshalled soldiers who had taken refuge in Königsberg and incorporated the Hitler Youth into the army. However, the 10,000 lightly wounded soldiers from the Fourth Army who had been sent to the already overcrowded hospitals of the city turned out to be of little use. This was the reason for the order to sixteen-year-olds to join regular soldiers and members of the Volkssturm in manning the twelve fortresses around the city.

Lasch ordered the Volkssturm to build yet more defences; endless trenches were constructed inside and outside the city. Foxholes were dug in the earth and minefields set out on the approaches to the city, under the watch of armed guards. Lasch established a main line of defence along the perimeter of the twelve outer forts of the city and he organised the preparation of interior defences along the girdle of inner forts built in the mid-nineteenth century. He also had defences put into the remains of the old royal castle, perched high above the River Pregel, which had been badly damaged by the British bombs the previous summer.

On 1 February, two days before the ultimatum to join the Volkssturm expired, Werner Terpitz fell into the hands of the SS. They discovered him in a queue outside a food shop:

... where I had gone in a pause in the shelling to buy food for my parents and grandparents. They hauled me out the queue, read through my papers, threatened me and told me not to wait until 3 February but to register with the Waffen-SS the following day.

This he did, signing up with a hundred other sixteen-year-olds all of whom:

> ... were united in our thoughts that we did not want to be in the Waffen-SS and no one wanted to be in the Volkssturm. We saw the SS as ideological and backward looking and the other no one took seriously.

They were given the uniforms of police cadets in an unusual green colour which 'fitted we thin-chested youths'. They were assigned to work with a Panzer division, although none of them knew who the Panzer troops were or what they did, and they were sent out to the suburb of Liep which was just five kilometres away from the Russian front line to do their training.

A few weeks earlier Guy Sajer, his battalion recalled to the defence of the Eastern Front, had come across a new Volkssturm unit like the one Werner Terpitz had joined:

> Now we were looking literally at children. Marching beside feeble old men. The oldest boys were about sixteen but there were others who could not have been more than thirteen. They had been hastily dressed in worn uniforms cut for men, and they were carrying guns, which were often as big as they were. They looked both comic and horrifying and their eyes were filled with unease, like the eyes of children at the reopening of school. Not one of them could have imagined the impossible ordeal that lay ahead.

Sajer and his battalion 'stood in profound silence, watching and listening to the final moments of this first adolescence. There was nothing else we could do.'[4]

On 20 February the siege of Königsberg was broken. The German Army retook the Samland Peninsula whilst the Königsberg garrison advanced and recaptured the suburb of Metgehen. When the German troops re-entered the area they found that many of the civilian population had been tortured and left for dead. Later one eyewitness recalled that the Russians had inflicted mass murder on the people of Metgehen:

> I saw women who were still wearing a noose around their necks that had been used to drag them to death. Often there were several tied together. I saw women whose heads were buried in the mire of a grave or in manure pits whose genitals bore the obvious marks of bestial cruelty.

In the next three weeks, 100,000 citizens and refugees took the opportunity to leave Königsberg for Pillau, via Metgehen. They were under constant Russian bombardment but they knew that from the port boatloads of citizens were being shipped westwards. So many were trying to escape that a temporary camp had to be set up in Peyse on the Königsberg maritime canal for the people streaming out of the city. There were few facilities and the freezing weather continued; hunger and sickness soon began to plague this temporary camp and some of the escapees tried to return to the city, feeling that at least there they would have some shelter and food. Despite opposition from Party officials, the military were prepared to allow those who wished to return to the city to do so. These returnees swelled the numbers in Königsberg who were to face the Russian onslaught a few weeks later.[5]

In February 1945 Dora Skopp and her family, who had been living in a rented house in the Königsberg suburb of Juditten, managed to get away. For weeks they had tried to fend off the freezing winter storms which constantly rattled at their doors and windows from which thick icicles hung. They had no fuel to keep themselves warm but they were not allowed to leave; only families with children were allowed to go unless they had special permission. Convinced they were going to die, they were surprised, late one night, to receive a phone call from an aunt that she had managed to get hold of papers which would allow them to leave on a munitions ship due to depart from the harbour in less than an hour. Dora and her mother would be able to go but her father would have to stay to help in the defence of the city. It was at least an hour on foot from where they lived to the docks and they would have to make their way in the dark through some of the most damaged and dangerous areas of the city. They hurriedly packed a few necessities, which they loaded on to a sledge, and dressed in their warmest clothes. They had no idea where the ship would be and were worried that they might not be able to cross the Pregel if the Reichsbahn Brücke had been opened to allow ships passage up the river. They met no one on the way, but it was a bright moonlit night and, after they had crossed the river safely, they found the ship, which had already cast off its moorings and was about to leave. The port was under constant artillery attack but, after a last emotional farewell to her father, Dora and her mother safely boarded the ship.

As it set off down the River Pregel, which was filled with such dangerous ice floes that headway seemed impossible, Dora took one last look at the city of her childhood. She saw the ruined houses covered with snow and in the background the burnt-out towers of the Castle from which the evening chorale had been played each night until Hitler's war had silenced it forever.[6]

Anneliese Drew's family also fled from Königsberg in February 1945; her mother could not take in the fact that everything had to be left behind. She took her leave of their apartment, making sure that every piece of furniture was arranged just as she liked it; then her husband took her by the hand and led her down the stairs. Their luggage had been packed for a week and they too loaded it onto a sledge and took it to the harbour. Anneliese, like Dora and so many thousands of others, kept her eyes on her father waving farewell on the quayside, getting smaller and smaller until they could see him no more. And then the truth hit them: that they had lost everything and her mother cried bitterly for the husband she had left behind.[7]

On 25 February, Werner Terpitz's family – his parents, grandparents and younger brothers – were given tickets to board a ship at the town harbour at 10.30 the following morning, although Werner had to stay behind to fight with the Volkssturm. When they reached the docks there was no boat and they were told to come again the following morning. On 27 February the *Greif* was waiting, moored at the Pregel docks. Despite there only being adequate room for 1,300 passengers, 2,200 were loaded on board. Leaving in the late afternoon, the *Greif* pushed its way through the ice floes on the Pregel and into the sea canal across the Haff. In the ice was the carnage of the previous day – the dead and the shipwrecks. The ship passed Pillau and struck out into the open sea towards Danzig.

They left Danzig two days later, on 1 March, on the *Eberhard Essberger* in terrible weather conditions. The sea was so rough that no refugees were allowed on deck, and everyone felt so seasick that it hardly mattered that there was little food available. With the weather worsening, the ship had to take shelter off-shore in order to ride out the storm. It was so cold that the breath of the cramped passengers condensed on the decks above them and formed icicles. Everyone was soaked to the skin and many of the passengers developed a fever. It took five days for the *Eberhard Essberger* to complete the short journey to Swinemünde, but when they arrived only wounded soldiers and Army recruits were allowed off. The refugees were kept on the ship for another twenty-four hours before being finally allowed to disembark. Forced to stay in Swinemünde for over a week to recover from the effects of their journey, the Terpitz family found themselves, on 13 March, in the midst of an attack on the Baltic port by Allied aircraft. It was a raid in which most of the town was destroyed and two ships loaded with refugees were sunk. Thousands of refugees waiting to be transported farther west were killed, although the Terpitz family survived and eventually managed to get on a train going west. Two and a half weeks after leaving Königsberg they reached relative safety at the small seaside town of Kuhlingsborn. They had travelled about 400 kilometres.[8]

In Königsberg the lull in the fighting allowed a semblance of normality to return. The bombing and artillery fire stopped and people came out of hiding; social life was resumed. The freezing weather abated in the middle of February and a warm spring breeze blew in from the sea. More and more people came in from the surrounding countryside and the city filled up with both civilians and retreating soldiers. Water, gas and electricity were restored and restaurants and cinemas reopened. Cattle were driven in from the country to provide milk and horses were killed to provide meat. The zoo even began to sell annual season tickets. But Erich Koch remained a baleful influence from his hideout. He kept the Volkssturm under strict Party control and Lasch was undermined at every opportunity. One suggestion, which may have come from Koch, was that the city should be defended by the Hitler Youth. All boys over the age of twelve were to muster at the

North Station to be trained, but the plan must have been quietly dropped since, after hanging round for many hours, they were sent home again. The official line was that there was to be no talk of surrender. Amongst the rubble and the damaged buildings were posters – 'Every House a Fortress', 'Königsberg Will Be the Grave of Bolshevism', and 'No Way Through'. A weary cynicism had set in amongst the people who remained in the town. People avoided the word 'military' and spoke less and less about 'army life'. Werner Terpitz recalls how they would simply say the single word '*Barras*' (army) making it sound hard and contemptuous. If someone said 'comrade' someone else would say, 'There are no comrades; they all fell at Stalingrad.' When they heard the Germans who had come to live in Königsberg from the Baltic States say, 'We want to make our home in the Reich' ('*Heim ins Reich*') the response was '*Wir wollen heim, uns reichts*' – 'We want to go home; we've had enough.' The young still managed to live from day to day with some optimism but the older people were deeply pessimistic, expecting exile to Siberia or death.[9] Many took refuge in alcohol and took such comfort as they could in their friends as they tried to ignore the deterioration in the city, the rubble, the rubbish, the dead horses, the abandoned trams.[10]

By the middle of March the Soviet Army was preparing for the final assault on Königsberg. The siege was expected to be one of the largest and most difficult urban assaults undertaken by the Soviet Army. Aerial inspections had shown how effective the preparations made in the last few months had been; the powerful forts, innumerable pillboxes and foxholes and well-constructed fortified buildings presented an enormous challenge. The city had three lines of defences; there were fifteen forts on the outer defences, a second line around the suburbs and another defensive line protected the inner city. In order to have a chance of success Marshal Vasilevsky, the commander of the operation who had taken over after Chernyakhovsky had been killed in January, had secured a promise from his high command that all Soviet aircraft operating in East Prussia together with all available heavy artillery would be on hand for use in the siege.

The planned operation consisted of three stages: the destruction of the German Fourth Army; the attack on Königsberg itself; and finally the annihilation of the German forces still holed up in the Samland Peninsula.

By this time everyone in Königsberg seemed nervous, expecting the final onslaught and the end of the city. It was impossible to imagine that the Russians would not want to destroy Königsberg, the jewel in East Prussia's crown, to avenge the horrors meted out at Stalingrad and Leningrad.

Full-scale fighting in East Prussia restarted on 13 March when the Third Belorussian Front broke through to the Baltic coast south-west of the city. The German Fourth Army was pushed steadily back to the sea and was forced into the Samland Peninsula near Pillau where it came under sustained Russian aerial attack. At first Hitler refused to allow the Fourth Army's men to be evacuated and kept them there until 26 March, only allowing them to go when their heavy equipment had been saved – a foolish decision which cost thousands of lives.

The Red Army now turned its attention again to Königsberg and towards the end of the month low-flying Russian aircraft began blaring out messages to the people of Königsberg: 'Men of the Volkssturm go home! We won't hurt you, you old granddads. Throw your rifles away.' Whenever the weather was clear their planes strafed the city and artillery fire increased steadily.

The preliminary bombardment began at the very beginning of April but the weather was poor, and fog and rain impeded pilots and gunners. April 1 was quiet but the next day the Russians began to use heavy artillery against the outer forts and pillboxes. On 4 April many listened to the news on the radio for the last time – then the electricity went off as the artillery bombardment grew in intensity.

Thursday 5 April 1945 was a beautiful warm spring day and the Russians used the clear blue skies and the sunshine to fly low above the city, dropping bombs as they went. Wave after wave of aircraft came over. Hans von Lehndorff observed that there was no response from the German armed services. 'We felt as if we were sailing on an ocean in a sinking ship,' he wrote.[11] The Soviet planes flew over undisturbed and attacked wherever took their fancy. A black pall of smoke hung over the inner city and floated up into the translucent sky. More than a hundred planes were in the sky at a time, most only 500 metres above the ground, so that they could deliberately aim at people in the streets. That day Werner Terpitz and his battalion were sent to defend the western edge of the city but it was already too late. Fortress Königsberg was indefensible.

The assault on Königsberg began the next day, at 7.30 a.m. on 6 April 1945. It began with the relentless shelling of the city by thousands of guns, mortars and rocket launchers, followed by yet more aerial bombardment. An eyewitness recorded:

> The city fell in ruins and burned. The German positions were smashed, the trenches ploughed up, embrasures were levelled with the ground, companies were buried, the signal systems torn apart and the ammunition stores destroyed. Clouds of smoke lay over the remnants of the houses of the inner city. On the streets were strewn fragments of masonry, shot-up vehicles and the bodies of horses and human beings.[12]

There were at this time about 130,000 civilians in the city who had to endure what General Lasch called 'the very image of terror'.[13]

The Russians had prepared well. They had spent the previous weeks making models of the defences of the city and identifying the weakest spots. When it started, the attack came from four Russian armies with 137,000 troops, 530 tanks and 2,400 aircraft, and a third of the entire Russian Air Force, ranged against a defending German Army of 35,000 men and about 50 tanks. The Russians were well-armed whilst the Germans, trying to hold back enemies on several fronts, had only four newly assembled divisions, plus the Volkssturm. The German Flak batteries lacked ammunition and the artillery power of the Soviets was overwhelming. General Lasch recalled that his troops 'had only enough ammunition for one day of fighting' and even this quantity was available only because they had been hoarding supplies. Two fleets of fighter aircraft blanketed the city with bombs and all the German communications were quickly destroyed. Under a constant hail of fire, soldiers and civilians huddled together in cellars.

As the Russians smashed through vital sections of the perimeter of the city, Lasch became convinced that the end was inevitable. Wave upon wave of air attacks passed over the city, which sank into burning ruins; not one German fighter plane was available to help resist the aerial bombardment. The German positions were crushed and the defenders' foxholes were overrun. Entire companies were buried and ammunition dumps were blown up. Both the Army and the Volkssturm were desperately short of equipment. They lacked weapons, ammunition and trained personnel to tell them what to do. On the streets the lack of anti-aircraft defence meant that there was a constant danger of being killed by the dive-bombers. Clouds of smoke hung over the city; the streets were littered with rubble and corpses; and terrified civilians fled from their bombed and burning houses, attempting to save whatever possessions they could. A survivor remembers with horror that:

> [The] Russian barrage on Königsberg was incredible. Even the old stagers had never seen anything like it. The youngest kids who were with us in the trenches screamed 'Help' and 'Mum' and the infantrymen were howling and bawling 'Get those kids out of the trenches.' It was a shambles.

German soldiers were urged by desperate civilians to stop fighting and bring the misery to an end but they were under orders not to surrender and fought on frantically.

Erich Schwarz, who was a youngster in the Volkssturm, thought this was right. 'It was obvious to us that we had to defend Königsberg. We weren't in the slightest doubt about that. It was our homeland.' But in the end he survived the battle because he went back to his command post with a message and found his commanding officer flirting with a Russian girl. He was so shocked that he went home, changed out of his uniform and gave up the fight.

The death struggle for *Festung Königsberg* was now at its height. The city was attacked by thousands of artillery weapons and squadrons of bombers circled endlessly, destroying everything they hit in, as Michael Wieck puts it, 'that wretched city'. Clouds of smoke hung over the town as chunks of buildings were sent flying through the air and cars were riddled with bullets. The Volkssturm was breaking apart and the wounded and the dead were piling up all over. Frightened civilians fled from the Russian infantry and tank corps; by the evening of 6 April 1945, Russian soldiers were already well into the city. Assault units had pushed their way in, blowing up several forts, cutting the Königsberg–Pillau railway line and piercing the defensive system. 'When I went outside,' wrote Hans von Lehndorff, 'the town was crawling with Russian soldiers with strange wild faces and the town was on fire.'[14] The attack continued throughout the night. Werner Terpitz was with a Panzer division when the fighting started on 6 April. His division was moved to a wood to the north of the city but it was so close to the advancing Russians that it was then moved to Gross Friedrichsberg, the estate where Gauleiter Koch had lived and amassed a huge fortune. It was now deserted but the soldiers found the Gauleiter's private bunker, full of weapons and ammunition, but they had found them too late. It was clear that defending Gross Friedrichsberg would not prevent the Red Army from taking Königsberg. Terpitz and his comrades waited there, terrified, until there was a cry that they should leave. 'Get out, the Ivans are here.'

After leaving Gross Friedrichsberg, he and his companions got away from the city on 7 April, hoping to make their way to the Frisches Haff. On the way Terpitz was seriously wounded in the leg by a splinter from a grenade. No one knew where a first-aid station was, or how near the Russians were, but eventually he was taken by military ambulance to Pillau where the Navy was making last efforts to get people away. He was treated and then put in an underground bunker where the beds of the injured were packed closely together. One by one the wounded were carried away to the ships until there were only three of four left. It was 12 April: 'We were all anxious, had we been forgotten?' And then he was left completely alone.

Eventually an attendant brought him some thin soup and told him that Königsberg had fallen. That afternoon Werner was taken to the port where he lay on a stretcher with other wounded soldiers on the quay waiting to be lifted on to a ship by crane – a terrifying and dangerous experience. 'As I was swung on I had a brief view of the harbour and the Haff and could say goodbye to this land where I would surely never live again.'

He was now on board the *Robert Bornholm*, laden with 1,700 wounded, 400 refugees and 100 soldiers, which reached Danish waters on 13 April. With Denmark still in German hands, they disembarked at Copenhagen and he was taken to a hospital at Aarhus to recover. He was allowed out on 2 May, to hear the news from Germany that Hitler had committed suicide two days earlier. Forced to confront what this meant Werner Terpitz wrote:

> In all the time I had been with soldiers I never met a dedicated Nazi. Most soldiers were not political; they saw the war as a German war, not a Nazi one. But there was the Führer, with his rasping voice, on the one hand challenging us with his caustic tone but on the other, like many psychopaths, undoubtedly with the gift of a kind of radiant charisma.

Many Germans were glad to see the back of Hitler and were glad that he and his *Parteibonzen* (Party big shots) had gone for good but Werner had to admit to himself:

> . . . that I, the son of a priest, the nephew of someone who had been a temporary prisoner of the Nazis, a notorious truant from the Hitler Youth, reacted with shock when I heard the news of Hitler's death. And when someone said, 'Good, I'm glad he's gone,' I felt that such a remark from someone involved in the fighting was quite irreverent. It was easier for older people, who had lived before Hitler, to accept a Germany without the Nazis.[15]

By the morning of 7 April, with the sound of battle at its height, Königsberg was covered in a thick pall of smoke, but this did not prevent more aircraft sweeping in to bomb yet more of the city. Some 246 bombers carried out three waves of attacks whilst ground troops made their way forward, street by street. They used 'Stalin organs', rocket launchers mounted on the backs of trucks, which could fire off rapid concentrated barrages. The number of German dead and wounded began to mount and the medical services could not cope. People began to hang white sheets out of their windows in the hope of bringing the conflict to an end before more lives were lost. On 8 April the Russians crossed the Pregel by boat, cutting off central Königsberg completely. Deputy Gauleiter Grossherr and the remaining Party personnel agreed that Königsberg was doomed and called on the military to organise a mass escape to Samland. Now, when it was all too late, enormous efforts were made to get people away with military help. General Lasch remembers how:

> Local knowledge ceased to be of any help in the inferno, which had once been the city of Königsberg. Ghostly lunar landscapes had come into being in place of the great avenues which used to lead through the city. Paths could be reconnoitred and just an hour later they were impassable; the remaining façades of the buildings collapsed into the streets and the ground was torn up by mighty bomb craters.[16]

About ninety per cent of the city was now destroyed.

The confusion was compounded when, at just after midnight on 9 April, the Party authorities, without reference to Lasch, passed the word for the civilian population to assemble on the old Pillau road. The people set off at 2.00 a.m. in a huge swarm. The Russians noticed and swamped the area with fire. The result was a bloodbath and heart-breaking scenes were played out as survivors tried to drag themselves back to their homes.

Daylight showed a city in ruins, enveloped in a cloud of smoke. Thousands were injured and the first-aid stations were overrun with people needing emergency treatment. The Russians were everywhere and treating the wounded became more and more difficult, as the attackers ransacked every building they came to, searching for valuables like watches and other treasures. On the morning of 9 April, Hans von Lehndorff, still working in the first-aid station where he was a doctor, was woken by the sound of Russian troops demanding that everyone should hand over their watches. The one German word they knew was watch – '*Uhr*' – and they trampled over the wounded shouting 'Ur, Ur, Ur'. When they found none, one of the soldiers stuck three fingers in the air and swore that if no one would give him a watch three people would be shot. The Russians had a saying: 'The first wave gets the wrist watches, the second wave gets the girls and women, the third wave gets what is left,' and these young soldiers were in the first wave.[17]

The writer Arno Surminski, who was born in East Prussia in 1934, also saw young soldiers in 1945 with rows of watches up each of their arms:

> To these youths from central and Asiatic Russia, watches were a valuable rarity. These lads had experienced nothing but hardship; they had lived off dried bread, slept in barns and marched for hundreds of kilometres. They had reached a part of Germany which had barely been touched by the war and the contrast with home was astounding to them.[18]

Most of these young soldiers were peasants and had never encountered prosperous houses full of furniture, china, clothes and jewellery; they were desperate to get their hands on any booty they could find. Many had never seen a bathroom or a lavatory and did not know how to use them and there are stories of young Soviet troops cladding themselves in women's lacy nightgowns and cavorting around the streets in their finery. Godfrey Lias, however, noticed that, 'In many cases the watches were thrown away or given away when they stopped because the looters did not know they needed winding.'[19]

That day General Lasch accepted that the situation was hopeless and contacted the Russian high command, who guaranteed good treatment. The surrender finally came on the evening of 9 April 1945 at 9.30. Hitler declared Lasch a traitor, sentenced him to death and ordered the arrest of his family. At the time of the surrender there were in the city between 30,000 and 35,000 soldiers, 15,000 foreign workers and more than 100,000 civilians

In Berlin, Helmut Altner read the news report which was posted daily in his divisional headquarters. It stated baldly:

> Königsberg Fortress was handed over to the Russians by General of Infantry Lasch. Despite this, parts of the loyal garrison have continued to resist. For surrendering to the enemy, General of Infantry Lasch has been condemned to death by hanging. His family has been arrested. Fighting on the western front in Nuremberg.

A small area of Königsberg did remain in the hands of the SS and military police and they held on for three more days in the Castle, the University and a few surrounding streets, until they had all been killed. Königsberg, the city from which Hitler had made his triumphant broadcast on 4 March 1933, was in the hands of the Russians.

On the morning of 10 April, the Russians ordered all civilians in the city to gather at the corner of Luisenallee and Hermanallee. They were threatening to set fire to any remaining intact parts of the city. Hans von Lehndorff was ordered out of the first-aid station and recalls how he had to pinch himself to make himself realise that what he was witnessing was not a nightmare. The beautiful city of his memories had been reduced to rubble, but in a waking dream he imagined that perhaps its beautiful buildings were still lying intact under the ruins. All around him the survivors of the siege crawled out of the ruins; most went meekly, along streets strewn with debris and pitted with bomb craters.

In the streets Soviet troops took watches and hand baggage and wandered through abandoned apartments and cellars looking for things to send home. They seized suitcases from survivors, frequently discarding the contents on the streets, for what they really wanted were empty bags to pack their booty.

When they reached the Luisenallee, the Germans were divided into groups. A few Jewish survivors were put into a group of their own and, after an interminable wait, were sent out of the city into the Samland Peninsula. As they left the city they again saw Königsberg on fire; the Russians had systematically set fire to any buildings which remained standing: 'When the flames blazed up to heaven the relentless stupidity and senselessness of everything that was happening left us numb'.[20] Others recall that the flames were so thick that it was impossible to see more than ten metres. Two days later they were taken back again to Königsberg, which was still smoking, to find everything burnt and 'ruins, nothing but ruins'. Likewise Lehndorff recalls how the city burned for days and that, despite the surrender, Soviet aircraft continued to bomb any building that remained standing.

The day after Königsberg surrendered, on 10 April 1945, the commander of the Third Belorussian Front, Vasilevsky, set up a central military command under Major-General Smirnov. His orders were to plan the 'clearance of enemy territory' of spies, enemy agents, terrorists and Nazi sympathisers. Russian soldiers swept the ruins looking for Nazis and surviving German soldiers were marched off to captivity in the labour camps whilst the Red Army troops plundered the city, burned, robbed, drank and raped. The intention was clearly to terrorise the remaining civilians; women's voices could be heard crying out 'Shoot me, shoot me' as they begged for mercy, and many shot or poisoned themselves to avoid the rage of the Russian soldiers. Many members of the Volkssturm who had survived the fall of their city were murdered.

Those who had reached safety in Germany found themselves part of a huge influx of approximately 15 million people who were expelled from Poland, Czechoslovakia and Hungary in the final weeks and the aftermath of the war. These *Heimatvertriebene* ('those expelled from their homeland') settled in both West and East Germany where a huge effort was made to integrate them into their new communities.

After Königsberg had fallen, the Soviet Army turned its attention to Pillau, which was fanatically defended by the Germans following orders which went out to hold the port at all costs in order to permit every available German ship to take off refugees and soldiers. Some 20,000 German troops fought furiously for six days, inflicting enormous damage on the Russians but with huge casualties on their own side. The Germans finally surrendered Pillau on 26 April 1945. As the war came to an end, the evacuation by ship of Army Group North stranded in Kurland also began. In an operation reminiscent of Dunkirk every available vessel, from minesweepers to trawlers, ran a shuttle service from tiny ports strung along the Kurland coast and took the soldiers to bigger harbours for evacuation to the likes of Kiel and Eckernförde.

The fate of the people of Königsberg had been exacerbated by the refusal of Gauleiter Koch to organise a proper evacuation before the Russians arrived and, as a result, the city was still crowded with soldiers, officials and civilians on the day of the surrender. Koch remained in East Prussia until 23 April when Pillau was just about to fall into Russian hands. The icebreaker *Ostpreussen*, the largest in the Königsberger fleet, had been waiting for weeks in Pillau harbour and the Gauleiter and his immediate entourage went aboard. The captain was ordered not to allow any civilians on board. Koch and his entourage arrived in Flensburg on 7 May, one day before Germany surrendered. Equipped with false papers, Koch hid in Hamburg, using the name Rolf Berger, where he was later arrested by the British and handed over to the Polish authorities in May 1949. Although he was condemned to death his sentence was commuted to life imprisonment for health reasons. He died in prison in Poland in 1986.

Koch had abandoned East Prussia and Königsberg and those who remained now faced the wrath of the Russians. The German armed forces had slaughtered indiscriminately in Russia and Eastern Europe and now it was the turn of the Red Army to exact its own revenge. Drunk on the alcohol they found in the town, Russian soldiers killed old men, raped women and set on fire what remained of the city. They ransacked cellars where people were hiding and destroyed the houses above their heads. They herded groups of people together and shot them; they stormed the hospitals and threw the sick and wounded out of the windows. People remember cemeteries being destroyed, gravestones ripped up, and coffins flung open. Anyone suspected of being a Nazi was rounded up and sent to a labour camp.[21]

Michael Wieck remembers how it seemed as if:

> These children of the steppes were probably encountering a modern city for the first time. Incited to frenzy, wild in their joy of victory, astonished at a

civilisation full of luxurious items, and drunk, they were beyond any control, they knew no bounds. They indulged every instinct be it sex, power, greed for possessions, gluttony or murder. If someone reproachfully pointed out to the Russians cruelly murdered people, they shrugged and told us of homes destroyed and all the atrocities. The Germans had cruelly murdered communists, commissars, Jews and partisans; they had starved Russian prisoners of war as well as obliterated cities and villages.

It was indeed a simple rough justice, for 'Whosoever attacks and defends as ruthlessly as the Germans did will be fought and vanquished with an equal absence of mercy.'[22]

In Berlin, Godfrey Lias indeed witnessed similar scenes:

When Berlin fell, the whole Russian Army went berserk and was allowed to do so by its commanders. Soldiers broke into houses, did what they liked to the inhabitants and carried off everything that was not too heavy or bulky.[23]

In Kurland, according to Gottlob Bidermann, news of the death of Hitler at the end of April was mostly received by the troops with indifference, though some breathed a sigh of relief:

During one of the nights shortly thereafter, a barrage broke forth from the enemy lines and after a short pause we heard the raucous voice of a Russian propagandist blaring from a loudspeaker 'Berlin is ours.'[24]

On 8 May, when Admiral Dönitz, Hitler's successor, finally surrendered to the allies Michael Wieck recalls the Russians 'exploding in an orgy of indescribable joy. The whole day they fired off everything they could shoot. Everyone was relieved that the madness was finally over.'[25] Now on his way to Berlin, N. K. Shneidmann saw similar scenes:

> The soldiers abandoned all rules of vigilance, instilled in them over the years of war, and gave vent to their instincts. The last day of the war a victory celebration in one of our detachments ended in disaster. Seven soldiers poisoned themselves with wood spirit. We could hardly believe that, after all the tribulations of war, one could face death at the hands of such a covert enemy as alcohol.[26]

Soldiers captured by the Red Army and the civilians of Königsberg who were considered fit were rounded up to be sent to labour camps in Russia. The transportation of East Prussian people to the USSR had started in 1944 and by mid-February 1945, several weeks before the fall of Königsberg, more than 28,000 had already been sent into the Soviet Union in order to strengthen the severely depleted Russian labour force. Many were taken first to Insterburg or Georgenburg as both these towns were near the Russian border and were railheads. From there they were then sent to Siberia, beyond the Ural Mountains. The journey took over two weeks in open carts and survivors recall their hunger and the way they were packed together so tightly that at first no one could stand up. They were given no food and many died from hunger or from typhus. Those who survived the journey were mainly those who had managed to bring a little of their own food with them. For the survivors, their internment in labour camps, where they did heavy jobs, particularly tree felling, lasted for four or five years. The majority did not return. In addition to taking labour, the Russians also dismantled what little machinery and industrial plant remained intact. Farms in the surrounding countryside were plundered.[27] The Russians seized stocks of cereals and potatoes and drove herds of cattle towards the Russian border.

Some civilians, like Wieck and his fellow Jewish survivors, were kept behind in the immediate aftermath of the surrender to drag corpses from where they had fallen and toss them into bomb craters. They were given ropes with a noose at one end which could be slung around the feet of the dead and used to drag the corpse.[28] Many people had committed suicide to escape the wrath of the Russians. Wieck found himself torn between the horror of what he found and the horror of Russian accounts of what the Germans had done to them. 'For the Russians there was only one enemy, the German invaders.'

Women, children and older men who were not considered fit to work in the camps were expelled from the city after enduring weeks of starvation and epidemics of dysentery and typhus. With all routes to the west closed, they were forced to scrape a living in the countryside around Königsberg. Others, who had been forcibly marched out of the city by the Russians, were brought back in again to live in former barracks where they slept on the floor in alphabetical order. There was no food and no sanitation and inevitably epidemics broke out. When people died, their bodies were thrown out of the windows.

One young wife was twenty-eight in March 1945 and four months pregnant. Her husband, like so many other men, had been forbidden to leave Königsberg, but on Good Friday, 30 March, she managed to get away from the city with her five-year-old son. At Pillau the weather was terrible; ice-breakers had to be used to break up metre-deep ice floes in the estuary before small tugs could take them to a waiting ship. After a few hours on board she was told that all were to disembark as the passage to the open sea would be too dangerous. Now, with thousands of other refugees, she had to make her way to the station at Rauschen in the hope that a train would take them to safety; as they made their way there they could see Königsberg burning in the distance.

When she got to Rauschen the Russians were already there. Some women were so frightened that they threw themselves and their children into the icy water – whilst others were seized by the Soviet troops and raped. She managed to find a hiding place for herself and her son but all night long she could hear the shrieks and cries of terrified women. At 5.00 a.m. the next day the Russians cleared the town and the women were forced to walk towards Palmnicken farther up the coast. Many grew weak and when they arrived there was no way to escape after all – the only choice was to be taken back to Königsberg in a lorry. She was taken as far as a deserted school where she was kept until late May before being returned to Königsberg. By this time the war was over and she crossed ravaged countryside where no one was left alive; she saw only the corpses of soldiers and animals rotting in the spring sunshine. Königsberg itself was a heap of rubble.

Not much is known about the eventual fate of the Königsbergers who were forced to stay in the city. Many committed suicide and those who hung on through the next few months, hoping for a return to normality which was never to come, were pre-occupied with finding enough food to live on. With no proper government in place a poorly disciplined army was left in charge of the city.[29] The Russians made no attempt to supply the German survivors with provisions. In an echo of what the people of Leningrad had had to endure when the Germans besieged their city, the people of Königsberg lived on the verge of starvation, amidst unburied corpses, non-existent sanitation, polluted water, disease and terrible infestations of flies. Stray dogs roamed the streets and anything that could be caught – cats, dogs, rats – ended up in the stew pot. On the brink of starvation and without fuel, survivors remember searching the gardens and fields for sorrel, dandelions and stinging nettles to boil into soup over fires made of sticks, seemingly unaware that the Germans had subjected the people of Leningrad to far worse. There was no electricity and even the polluted water supplies often failed.

The Russianisation of Königsberg began even before the final surrender on 8 May 1945. Loudspeakers were installed on every corner which blared out Russian music. Within a few days of the fall of the city, direction signs and place names in German were torn down and replaced by new ones in Russian script. As Russians arrived in the town, those Germans who still had somewhere to live were turned out of their homes and forced to find shelter in bombed-out cellars without heating, lighting or water.

In the winter of 1945–6 there were rumours of cannibalism and in the summer of 1946 there were outbreaks of typhus, malaria and typhoid, caused by drinking water from artificial lakes (built by the Nazis to double the water supply) being filled with decaying corpses and garbage. There were terrible infestations of lice and rats. The only proper food available, apart from a small allowance of bread given to those Germans who were given jobs by the Russians, was rye grain from fields in the surrounding countryside that had not been harvested in the summer of 1945 and had regrown a season later.

Of those who stayed behind, it is thought that half died in the course of the first three months after the surrender and another twenty-five per cent in the next three years. Michael Wieck believes that the Russians '. . . intentionally destroyed every resource needed for survival and thwarted every attempt people made to look after themselves, as if they wanted to accelerate the rate at which Königsbergers died.' And this was because, 'In their hearts they carried the pain of millions and millions of fallen comrades, starving civilians and murdered relatives and friends.'[30]

In July 1946 northern East Prussia and Königsberg, an area about half the size of Belgium, officially became part of the Soviet Union after the signing of an agreement at the inter-Allied Potsdam Conference, which met in July and August 1945. The rest of East Prussia would go to Poland; Memel and the surrounding countryside became part of Lithuania. Königsberg and its environs were collectively renamed the Kaliningrad *Oblast* (region) in July 1946 (after Mikhail Kalinin, one of Stalin's cronies who had just died) and it was declared a military zone. A barbed-wire fence was erected along its entire border with Poland, dividing families and communities. The first Soviet settlers arrived that summer from many parts of Russia, and East Prussia started to become Russian. Banners displaying the faces of Stalin, Lenin, Marx and Kalinin appeared all over the remains of the city and loudspeakers played Russian music. The port of Pillau was renamed Baltiysk and became home to the Soviet Baltic Fleet. It is still closed to foreigners and is the only Russian Baltic port which is ice-free for most of the winter. During the Cold War there were at times up to half a million troops stationed in the Kaliningrad region although there have been fewer since the end of the Cold War.

The German name of each village and town was changed and, unlike in Poland where many place names were translated literally and directly (so that, for example, Frauenburg became Frombork), entirely new names were invented. Insterburg, the second largest town in East Prussia was renamed Chernyakhovsk and Paul Terpitz's parish of Nordenburg was renamed Krylovo although little remains of the small town today except the ruins of the church tower where 'jackdaws fly around and the storks still nest'. Crows nest in the remains of the chancel.

In 1946 the remaining Germans in the *oblast* thought they might be able to start to rebuild their lives in their homeland. They were permitted to have their own German-language newspaper, a German-speaking school was started, and an orphanage was set up for children who had lost their parents.[31] However, in October 1947 the Russian authorities announced that they were all to be required to leave in the next few months. All remaining Germans in Königsberg were to be deported to Germany in special trains or be sent to Soviet labour camps; property that had previously belonged to them was officially confiscated. Michael Wieck and his parents, for example, managed to get passes to leave in April 1948.

Some of those who experienced the evacuation of 1947–8 recall taking a last look at the old city. One family wandered through the ruined streets to the Litzenstrasse where they had once lived. Not one house was left standing and the city library was in ruins, surrounded by burnt paper half a metre deep. In the Kaiser Wilhelm Platz there was an uncanny hush – there was no one in the once bustling square, although the statues of both Wilhelm I and Bismarck were still standing. The Castle beyond was a burnt-out shell. On the Kneiphof, the grammar school which Werner Terpitz had attended and the University were both mere heaps of ashes. By the remains of the Cathedral they found that the Kant memorial was intact and the coat of arms of Albert, the founder of the University, lay undamaged on the ground. Inside the Cathedral there was little left except a black ragged cloth fluttering in the breeze from the post of what had been the pulpit. Elsewhere there was virtually nothing left except empty, open cellars and scenes of waste and desolation. Everywhere there was an 'unbearable silence' which was interrupted by some suspicious Russian soldiers who demanded to know what they were doing.

They left Königsberg on 30 October 1947, with 2,500 others in a goods train of over fifty wagons. Such trains moved slowly, often standing still for longer than they moved and this one took eight days to cross Poland and to enter East Germany. Königsberg Castle was not finally destroyed until the 1960s. The local authorities had been longing to be rid of it and in the end Moscow's permission came in 1969. The remains of the building were dynamited, then it was bulldozed and soldiers took away the rubble. In its place the Kaliningrad government built a hideous twenty-storey monstrosity called the House of the Soviets. The building was never completed and has never been used. It still has broken windows, broken walls and stairs without treads. In 1976 the Lutherkirche, a beautiful neo-Renaissance building which had survived the war, was deliberately destroyed. In the late 1980s some Germans returned from the areas to which they had been deported and there are now around 10,000 Germans living amongst a Russian population of well over a million.

After 1990 the Kaliningrad *Oblast* became an 'exclave' with no land connection to the rest of Russia. With the collapse of the Soviet Union and the independence of the surrounding Baltic States, Kaliningrad had become an impoverished province cut off from the rest of the Russian Federation by Poland, Belarus and Lithuania. With the enlargement of the European Union on 1 May 2004, its isolation became complete.

Officially there are now only ten major buildings from Prussian times left in Kaliningrad. Of the thirty-four churches, four remain. The city gates still stand in the thick city walls which not even the Russians could destroy – the Brandenburg gate, the Sackheim gate and four others. The old concert hall, the Stadthalle, is still there, as is the light-blue-painted Bourse, the former Stock Exchange. The old trade fair site, the *Ostmesse*, is now the Central Market. There are no graves and no memorials to commemorate those Germans who died during the Soviet siege. In the suburbs some of the villas of the German middle classes remain standing. The buildings around the Cathedral on the Kneiphof are all gone, as is most of the old town, the Altstadt. Today these areas are mostly open spaces of scrubby grass and straggly trees. In the countryside, around 300 abandoned German villages which had engaged in farming before the war have never been resettled and land that was once the granary of the eastern Baltic lies fallow.

The impression that old Königsberg is still intangibly there under the wreckage of Kaliningrad frequently recurs. Amos Elon visited Kaliningrad in 1999 and conjured up a vision strangely similar to the old legend of Winetha and the impressions of Hans von Lehndorff in April 1945:

> One cannot escape an uncanny feeling of the existence of the old Königsberg, like the negative of a damaged photograph, lying ten to twenty feet underneath the city's surface, covered with rubble from the war and Stalin's bulldozers. If the huge mass of debris were cleared away, the old topography, now flattened out, would come into view, with its natural hills and dips, its landscaped river basins and embankments.[32]

In the summer months the German tourists come to Kaliningrad, though they still call it Königsberg They look round the new Russian Orthodox Cathedral, which is near completion, and go to the few shops in the town centre which have been revitalised. They visit the Cathedral on the Kneiphof, which is very slowly being restored with German money, and the Cathedral Museum which has been established in the South Tower. They are able to see the tomb of Immanuel Kant, which survived the war. The Island swarms with traders selling ice creams and Coke. Naturally they also sell views of old Königsberg and picture guides and plans in German and Russian.

Many of these visitors are elderly and their memories of the old city are affectionate; most have no expectation that it will ever be German again, but they show little real understanding of the reasons for its destruction. Their memoirs rarely mention the brutality of the German invasion of the Soviet Union, the millions of Russian dead and the laying waste of the lands which the German Army invaded. They muse on the loss of their *'Heimat'* and the undeniably dreadful experiences of the evacuation of the East Prussians from their homeland. Yet most have erected a veil which prevents them from accepting that the destruction of Königsberg and the loss of East Prussia were the consequence of Nazism and most particularly the cruelties meted out to the people of Russia by the German armed forces and the Nazi leadership.

The manner in which the people of East Prussia had to flee and the fate of those who stayed behind were the direct result of German conduct during the war. Hitler's refusal to countenance an orderly evacuation meant that the Germans of East Prussia and the citizens of the once beautiful city of Königsberg became both his victims and part of his final sacrifice.

Notes

Chapter One A Land of Quiet Austerity (pp. 25–35)

1. Old Prussian song, text Erich Hannighofer, *Land der dunkeln Wälder und kristallen Seen*.
2. Sybil Bannister, *I Lived under Hitler*, London, 1957, p. 58.
3. Maria Gräfin von Dönhoff, *Kindheit in Ostpreussen*, Berlin, 1998, p. 104.
4. Ernst Wiechert, *The Simple Life*, Munich, 1954, p. 286.
5. Max Fürst, *Gefilte Fisch: Eine Jugend in Königsberg*, Stuttgart, 2001, p. 55.
6. Gertrud Papendick, Foreword to Anon., *Königsberg in 144 Bildern*, Hamburg, 1964.
7. The Teutonic Knights (*Deutscher Orden*) were originally a German crusading order formed in Palestine in the twelfth century. They later turned their attentions to eastern Europe and took over northern Poland in 1225 from where they moved on to Königsberg.
8. Sebastian Wormell (ed.), *Poland*, Pallas, 2002, p. 403.
9. Neil Taylor *et al.*, *Baltic Capitals Bradt Travel Guide*, Chalfont St Peter, 2001, p. 175.
10. *Nun ruhen alle Wälder*, text Paul Gerhardt, 1647, melody Heinrich Isaac, 1450–1517.
11. Papendick, Foreword.
12. Wilhelm Matull, *Liebes Altes Königsberg*, Munich, 1957, p. 25.
13. The mathematical puzzle, the Seven Bridges of Königsberg, was first posed by the mathematician Leonhard Euler (1707–83). The question asked: was it possible to cross all the bridges exactly once and return to the starting point?
14. The Hanseatic League was a league of merchant traders which operated mainly in the cities and ports of Northern Germany and the Eastern Baltic. It was protectionist and it controlled the trade of most of the commodities exchanged in the region.
15. Baedeker Guide, *Northern Germany*, 1900, p. 224.

16. Max Fürst, who grew up in Königsberg, recalls that every school child had to visit the Kant memorial and copy out these words at least once in their school career.

17. Wilhelm Matull, *Damals in Königsberg, 1919–23*, Munich, 1998, p. 44.

Chapter Two The Shameful Peace *(pp. 36–43)*

1. Richard Bessel, *Germany after the First World War*, Oxford, 1993, p. 85.
2. Fritz Gause, *Geschichte des Preussenlandes*, Rautenberg, 1966, p. 84.
3. Baedeker, p. 216.
4. Bannister, p. 24.
5. Dönhoff, *Namen die keiner mehr nennt*, Munich, 1964, p. 49.
6. The Freikorps was a collection of private armies made up of demobilised soldiers and secretly financed and equipped by the German High Command after the end of the First World War.
7. Jürgen Manthey, *Königsberg*, Munich, 2005, p. 558.
8. Gause, p. 88.

Chapter Three Voting for the Nazis *(pp. 44–54)*

1. Old Prussian song.
2. Dönhoff, *Kindheit in Ostpreussen*, p. 66.
3. Philip Dwyer, *Modern Prussian History, 1830–1947*, London, p. 159.
4. Thomas Childers, *The Nazi Voter: The Social Foundations of Nazism*, North Carolina, 1993, pp. 47–150.
5. Gause, p. 189.
6. Alan Bullock, *Hitler: A Study in Tyranny*, London, 1952, p. 152.
7. Quoted in Martin Wanh, *Hitler and the Holocaust: The Hidden Story*, Philadelphia, 2001, p. 234.
8. Count Harry Kessler, *Diaries of a Cosmopolitan*, London, 2000, pp. 396–8.
9. Childers, *The Nazi Voter*, contains a detailed analysis of voting patterns in the elections between 1929 and 1933.
10. <www.hitler.org/speeches>.
11. Cited in <www.spartacus-schoolnet.co.uk>.

Chapter Four A Fresh Beginning *(pp. 55–63)*

1. Lorenz Grimoni (ed.), *Königsberg, 750 Years*, Duisburg, 2005, p. 76.
2. Erich Koch was one of two suggested for the post of Gauleiter, the other was Heinrich Himmler. Koch had started his career as a railway worker in Elberfeld in the Ruhr where he had joined the Nazi Party.
3. Grimoni, p. 75.
4. Dora Ferle-Skopp, *Über die Hönigbrücke*, Munich, 1993, p. 33.
5. Bullock, p. 265.

6. Victor Klemperer, *The Klemperer Diaries: I Shall Bear Witness, 1933–4*, Phoenix, 1999, p. 647.
7. Helga Gerhardi, *Helga*, Aylesbury, 1993, p. 17.
8. Ferle-Skopp, p. 39.
9. Manthey, p. 647.
10. Gause, p. 190.
11. Marianne Mackinnon, *The Naked Years*, London, 1989, p. 43.
12. 'Black treasure' is a reference to the coal of the Saar. This version is the one remembered by Marianne Mackinnon, but other wordings of the verse also exist.
13. Martin Bergau, *Der Junge von der Bernsteinküste*, Heidelberg, 1994, p. 17.
14. Michael Wieck, *A Childhood under Hitler and Stalin*, Wisconsin, 2003, pp. 29–30.
15. Hitler's speech in Königsberg was on 25 March 1938; cited in <www.adolfhitler.ws.lib>.

Chapter Five The Jews of Königsberg *(pp. 64–74)*

1. Fürst, p. 84.
2. Gabrielle Lesser, *Centropa Quarterly*, vol. 6, winter 2004.
3. Walther Rathenau was a founder of the German Democratic Party. He became Minister of Reconstruction in the Weimar government in 1921 and was appointed Foreign Minister in 1922. He believed that Germany should fulfil its Versailles commitments and also attempted a rapprochement with the USSR. He was assassinated by two right-wing Freikorps officers in Berlin.
4. Kessler, p. 399.
5. Manthey, p. 639.
6. Wieck, p. 40.
7. Wieck, pp. 42–3.
8. Gerhardi, p. 25.
9. Ferle-Skopp, p. 104.
10. Ferle-Skopp, p. 148.
11. Wieck, p. 18.
12. Gerhardi, p. 23.
13. Ferle-Skopp, p. 50.
14. Wieck, p. 63–4.
15. Ferle-Skopp, p. 154.
16. Wieck, p. 66.

Chapter Six The War *(pp. 75–96)*

1. Hitler, speech to Reichstag, 28 April 1939.
2. Albert Forster speech, 16 September 1939, <www.kki.net.pl>.
3. Bannister, p. 59.

4. Bannister, p. 64.
5. William Harbutt Dawson, *Germany under the Treaty*, London, 1933.
6. Grimoni, p. 76.
7. Bergau, p. 21.
8. Ferle-Skopp, p. 115.
9. Agnes Marie Grisebach, *Eine Frau Jahrgang 13*, Hamburg, 2001.
10. von der Groeben, 'Jugendzeit in Ostpreussen', <www.geocities.com/ jugendzeitostpr>.
11. Sarah Collins *The Alien Years*, London, 1949, p. 107.
12. Howard K. Smith, *Last Train from Berlin*, London, 1942, p. 42.
13. Gerhardi, p. 74.
14. Smith, p. 119.
15. Mackinnon, pp. 147–8.
16. Mackinnon, p. 150.
17. Collins, p. 137.
18. Gerhardi, p. 99.
19. Olaf Nissen, *Germany Land of Substitute*s, London, 1944, p. 48.
20. Gerhardi, p. 79.
21. Bergau, p. 36.

Chapter Seven As You Sow . . . *(pp. 113–23)*

1. Smith, p. 106.
2. Hitler, *Mein Kampf*, Hurst & Blackett edn., London, 1939, p. 360.
3. Quoted in Michael Burleigh, *Germany Turns Eastward*, London, 1988, p. 149.
4. *Ibid.*, pp. 62–7.
5. Robert Solomon Wistrich, *Who's Who in Nazi Germany*, London, 2001, p. 120.
6. James Lucas, *War on the Eastern Front*, London, 1998, p. 16.
7. Heinrich Himmler, speech made at Posen, 4 October 1943; cited in <www.ess.uwe.ac.uk>.
8. Godfrey Lias, *I Survived*, London, 1954, p. 19.
9. Harrison L. Salisbury, *The 900 Days: The Siege of Leningrad*, London, 2000, pp. 291–2.
10. *Ibid.*, p. 386.
11. *Ibid.*, p. 387.
12. *Ibid.*, p. 446.
11. *Ibid.*

Chapter Eight Under-Estimating the Colossus *(pp. 124–53)*

1. For a full account see Richard Overy, *Russia's War*, London, 1997, Chapter 2, 'The Hour before Midnight'.
2. Overy, *Russia's War*, p. 71.

3. Gottlob Herbert Bidermann, *In Deadly Combat*, Kansas, 2000, Chapter 2.
4. Arvid Fredborg, *Behind the Steel Wall*, London, 1944, p. 33.
5. Franz Halder, *Kriegstagebuch*, Vol. 3, Stuttgart, 1964, entry for 11 August 1941.
6. Gerhardi, pp. 76–7.
7. Smith, p. 56.
8. Fredborg, p. 48.
9. *Ibid.*.
10. Bernt Engelmann, *In Hitler's Germany: Everyday Life in the Third Reich*, London, 1988, p. 223.
11. Smith, pp. 61–4.
12. Smith, pp 76–7.
13. Fredborg, p. 49.
14. Smith, pp 76–7.
15. Smith, p. 65.
16. Halder, *Kriegstagebuch*, entry for 2 October 1941.
17. Fredborg, p. 68.
18. Overy, *Russia's War*, p. 161.
19. Overy, *Why the Allies Won*, p. 277.
20. Overy, *Why the Allies Won*, p. 74.
21. Overy, *Russia's War*, p. 138.
22. Joachim Wieder & Heinrich Graf von Einsiedel, *Stalingrad: Memories and Re-assessments*, 1962, p. 30.
23. Wieder, p. 67.
24. Smith, p. 243.
25. Wieder, p. 82.
26. Cited in <www.users.pandora.be/stalingrad>, entry for 22 January 1943.
27. Overy, *Russia's War*, p. 185.
28. Marion Gräfin von Dönhoff, *Namen die keiner mehr nennt*, p. 4.
29. Harry Mielert letters quoted in Stephen G. Fritz, *The German Soldier in the Second World War*, Kentucky, 1995, p. 111.
30. Lucas, *War on the Eastern Front*, p. 80.
31. Peter G. Tsouras (ed.), *Fighting in Hell*, New York, 1995, p. 58.
32. Tsouras, pp. 115–19.
33. Cf. John Erickson, *The Road to Berlin*, London, 1983, Chapter 9.
34. Gordon Craig, *Germany 1866–1945*, Oxford, 1978, p. 754.
35. Sajer, *The Forgotten Soldier*, London, 1999, p. 376.
36. Guy Sajer, p. 376.
37. Cf. Bidermann, Chapter 9, 'The Coming Storm'.
38. Sajer, p. 439.
39. Bidermann, p. 226.

Chapter Nine The Time for Repayment *(pp. 154–84)*

1. Cf. Alfred M. de Zayas, *Nemesis at Potsdam*, London, 1997, Chapter 3.
2. de Zayas, p. 11.
3. de Zayas, p. 90.
4. de Zayas, p. 57.
5. Admiral Karl Dönitz, *Memoirs*, London, 1958, p. 430.
6. Guido Knopp, *Die Grosse Flucht*, Munich, 2002, Foreword.
7. de Zayas, p. 14.
8. Mackinnon, p. 167.
9. Bergau, p. 59.
10. Christopher Duffy, *Red Storm on the Reich*, London, 1991, p. 14.
11. Herbert Reinoss (ed.), *Letzte Tage in Ostpreussen*, Augsburg, 1999, p. 320.
12. Dönhoff, *Namen die keiner mehr kennt*, p. 20.
13. Wieck, p. 103.
14. Werner Terpitz, *Wege aus dem Osten*, Munich, 1997, pp. 34–5.
15. Wieck, p. 105.
16. Ferle-Skopp, p. 192.
17. Grimoni, p. 81.
18. Bidermann, pp. 246–8.
19. Matthew Hughes and Chris Mann, *Inside Hitler's Germany*, London, 2004, p. 170.
20. Helmut Altner, *Berlin Dance of Death*, Staplehurst, 2002, p. 6.
21. Dönhoff, *Namen die keiner mehr kennt*, p. 15.
22. Otto Schneidereit, *Zwischen Zwei Weltkriegen*, Berlin, 1999, pp. 267–9.
23. Hans Graf von Lehndorff, *Ostpreussisches Tagebuch*, Munich, 1967, p. 6.
24. Dönhoff, *Namen die keiner mehr kennt*, p. 14.
25. Sajer, chap. 17.
26. Knopp, pp. 41–3.
27. G. K. Koschorrek, *Blood Red Snow*, London, 2002, p. 293.
28. James Charles Roy, *The Vanished Kingdom: Travels Through the History of East Prussia*, Colarado, 1999, p. 287.
29. Schneidereit, p. 277.
30. Wieck, p. 109.
31. Lehndorff, p. 10.
32. Gerhardi, p. 188.
33. Gerhardi, p. 175.
34. Lehndorff, p. 10.
35. Downdraft gasifiers, invented by a Swede, Torsten Kalle, were widely used in World War II to provide fuel for vehicles.

36. Lehndorff, p. 10.
37. Dönhoff, *Namen die keiner mehr kennt*, p. 20.
38. Terpitz, pp. 38–9.
39. Bidermann, p. 260.
40. Lali Horstmann, *Nothing for Tears*, London, 1953, p. 36.

Chapter Ten 'A Vast Flood of Human Misery' *(pp. 185–208)*
1. Erickson, *The Road to Berlin*, p. 431.
2. Dieckert and Grossman, *Der Kampf um Ostpreussen*, Munich, 1960, p. 72.
3. Overy, *Russia's War*, p. 257.
4. de Zayas, p. 65.
5. Dieckert and Grossman, p. 82.
6. Cited in <www.kriegsende.ard.de>.
7. Knopp, p. 59.
8. Knopp, p. 74.
9. Lias, p. 76.
10. Dieckert and Grossman, p. 121.
11 Knopp, p. 63.
12. Quoted in Douglas Botting, *In the Ruins of the Reich*, London, 2005, p. 91.
13. Dönhoff, *Namen die keiner mehr kennt*, pp. 22–3.
14. Sajer, p. 526.
15. Sajer, p. 526.
16. Dönitz, p. 432.
17. Lehndorff, p. 16.
18. Dieckert and Grossman, p. 104.
19. Wieck, p. 113.
20. Sajer, p. 530.
21. Gerhardi, p. 210.
22. Gerhardi, p. 215.
23. Mackinnon, 193.
24. The full story can be found in Guido Knopp, *Der Untergang der Gustloff*, Munich, 2002.
25. Reminiscences of Karl Hoffmann, quoted in <www.wilhelmgust loff.com>.
26. Bannister, p. 195.
27. Bergau, p. 195.
28. Roy, p. 242.
29. N. K. Shneidmann, *Jerusalem of Lithuania*, Oakville, Ontario, 1995, p. 139.
30. Terpitz, pp. 56–7.
31. Terpitz, p. 53. The verse of the Bible cited reads: 'For here we have no lasting city, but we are looking for the city that is to come.'

32. Terpitz, p. 53.
33. Terpitz, p. 46.

Chapter Eleven Fortress Königsberg *(pp. 209–40)*

1. Terpitz, p. 69.
2. Terpitz, p. 69
3. Terpitz, pp. 70–1.
4. Sajer, p. 473.
5. Dieckert and Grossman, *op. cit.*
6. Ferle-Skopp, p. 205.
7. Annaliese Drew, *Meine Flucht aus Königsberg*, Berlin, 1998, p. 8.
8. Terpitz, pp. 81–3.
9. Terpitz, p. 86.
10. Hans Deichelmann, *Ich sah Königsberg sterben*, Dortmund, 2000, p. 9.
11. Lehndorff, pp. 59–60.
12. Wieck, p. 125.
13. Reinos, pp. 113–14.
14. Lehndorff, p. 61.
15. Terpitz, pp. 111–12.
16. Lasch's own account of the fall of the fortress city is included in Reinos, pp. 113–43.
17. Lehndorff, pp. 111–12.
18. Arno Surminski, *Klein schöner Land*, Munich, 1991.
19. Lias, pp. 64–5.
20. Wieck, p. 140.
21. Ruth Kibelka, *Ostpreussens Schicksalsjahre 1944–48*, Berlin, 2004, p. 45.
22. Wieck, pp. 136–7.
23. Lias, p. 76.
24. Bidermann, p. 281.
25. Wieck, p. 160.
26. Shneidmann, p. 140.
27. Kibelka, p. 44.
28. Wieck, p. 144.
29. Kibelka, p. 186.
30. Wieck, p. 167.
31. Grimoni, pp. 81–2.
32. Roy, Foreword.

Appendix

PLACE NAMES

Places mentioned in the text are given their German names. Many of these are now in Russia, Poland or Lithuania and their modern names are given below (German names first).

Allenburg	Druzhba	Libau	Liepaja
Allenstein	Olsztyn	Marienwerder	Kwidzyn
Braunsberg	Braniewo	Marienburg	Malbork
Breslau	Wroclaw	Memel	Klaipeda
Bromberg	Bydgoszcz	Metgehen	Lesnoye
Cranz	Zelenogradsk	Nemmersdorf	Mayakovskoye
Cracow	Krakow	Nemionen	Golovkino
Danzig	Gdansk	Neukuhren	Pionersky
Darkehmen	Ozyorsk	Nidden	Nida
Elbing	Elblag	Nordenburg	Krylovo
Eydtkuhen	Chernyshevskoye	Palmnicken	Yantarny
Frauenburg	Frombork	Pilkallen	Dobrovolsk
Friedrichstein	Kamenka	Pillau	Baltiysk
Georgenburg	Mayovka	Polangen	Palanga
Gotenhafen	Gdynia	Posen	Poznan
Gross Friedrichsberg		Quittainen	Kwitajny
	Zakrzewo	Rastenburg	Ketrzyn
Gumbinnen	Gusev	Rauschen	Svetlogorsk
Haselberg	Krasnyznamensk	Rositten	Rybachy
Heiligenbeil	Mamonovo	Schlossberg	Dobrovolsk
Heydekrug	Silute	Schwirwindt	Kutusowo
Insterburg	Chernyakhovsk	Stettin	Szczecin
Juditten	Mendeleevo	Stutthof	Sztutowo
Kattowitz	Katowice	Tannenberg	Stebark
Königsberg	Kaliningrad	Tilsit	Sovetsk
Labiau	Polessk	Wehlau	Znamensk

BIBLIOGRAPHY

Anon., *Königsberg in 144 Bildern*, Hamburg, 1964

Anon., *Northern Germany*, Baedeker Guide 1900

Altner, Helmut, *Berlin Dance of Death*, Staplehurst, 2002

Baedeker Guyide, *Northern Germany*, 1900 edition

Bannister, Sybil, *I Lived under Hitler*, London, 1957

Bergau, Martin, *Der Junge von der Bernsteinküste*, Heidelberg, 1994

Bessel, Richard, *Germany after the First World War*, Oxford, 1993

Bidermann, Gottlob, *In Deadly Combat*, Kansas, 2000

Bullock, Alan, *Hitler, a Study in Tyranny*, London, 1952

Burleigh, Michael, *Germany Turns Eastward*, London, 1988

Childers, Thomas, *The Nazi Voter: The Social Foundations of Fascism in Germany, 1919–1933*, North Carolina, 1988

Collins, Sarah, *The Alien Years*, London, 1949

Craig, Gordon, *Germany 1866–1945*, Oxford, 1978

Dawson, William Harbutt, *Germany under the Treaty*, London, 1933

Deichelmann, Hans, *Ich sah Königsberg sterben*, Dortmund, 2000

Dieckert and Grossman, *Der Kampf um Ostpreussen*, Munich, 1960

Dönhoff, Marian Gräfin von, *Namen die keiner mehr nennt*, Munich, 1964

————, *Kindheit in Ostpreussen*, Berlin, 1998

Dönitz, Karl, *Memoirs*, London, 1958

Drews, Annaliese, *Meine Flucht aus Königsberg*, Berlin, 1998

Duffy, Christopher, *Red Storm on the Reich*, London, 1991

Dwyer, Philip (ed.), *Modern Prussian History, 1830–1947*, London, 2001

Elon, Amos, *The Pity of It All: A Portrait of Jews in Germany, 1743–1933*, London, 2004

Engelmann, Bernt, *In Hitler's Germany: Everyday Life in the Third Reich*, London, 1988

Erickson, John, *The Road to Berlin*, London, 1983

Ferle-Skopp, Dora, *Über die Hönigbrücke. Kindheit und Jugend in Königsberg*, Munich, 1993

Fredborg, Arvid, *Behind the Steel Wall*, London, 1944

Fritz, Stephen G., *The German Soldier in the Second World War*, Kentucky, 1995

Fürst, Max, *Gefilte Fisch: Eine Jugend in Königsberg*, Stuttgart, 2001

Gause, Fritz, *Geschichte des Preussenlandes*, Munich, 1966

Gerhardi, Helga, *Helga*, Aylesbury, 1993

Grimoni, Lorenz (ed.), *Königsberg, 750 Years*, Duisburg, 2005

Grisebach, Agnes Marie, *Eine Frau Jahrgang 13*, Hamburg, 2001

Halder, Franz, *Kriegstagebuch*, Vol. 3, Stuttgart, 1964

Horstmann, Lali, *Nothing for Tears*, London, 1953

Hughes M., and Mann C., *Inside Hitler's Germany: Life under the Third Reich*, London, 2004

Kershaw, Ian, *Hitler, 1936–1945, Nemesis*, London, 2000

Kessler, Count Harry, *The Diaries of a Cosmopolitan, 1918–37*, London, 2000

Kibelka, Ruth, *Ostpreussens Schicksalsjahre, 1944–48*, Berlin, 2004

Klemperer, Victor, *The Klemperer Diaries: I Shall Bear Witness, 1933–4*, Phoenix, 1999

Knopp, Guido, *Die Grosse Flucht*, Munich, 2002

——, *Der Untergang der Gustloff*, Munich, 2002

Koschorrek, G. K., *Blood Red Snow*, London, 2002

Lehndorff, Hans Graf von, *Ostpreussisches Tagebuch, 1945–47*, Munich, 1967

Lias, Godfrey, *I Survived*, London, 1954

Lucas, James, *War on the Eastern Front: The German Soldier in Russia, 1941–1945*, London, 1979

——, *The Last Year of the German Army, May 1944–May 1945*, London, 1994

Mackinnon, Marianne, *The Naked Years: A Young Girl's experiences in Nazi Germany*, London, 1987

Manthey, Jürgen, *Königsberg. Geschichte einer Weltbürgerrepublick*, Munich, 2005

Matull, Wilhelm, *Damals in Königsberg 1919–1939*, Munich, 1998

———, *Liebes altes Königsberg*, Würzburg, 2004

Nissen, Olaf, *Germany Land of Substitutes*, London, 1944

Overy, Richard, *Why the Allies Won*, London, 1996

———, *Russia's War*, London, 1997

Reinoss, Herbert (ed.), *Letzte Tage in Ostpreussen*, Augsburg, 1999

Roy, James Charles, *The Vanished Kingdom, Travels through the History of East Prussia*, Colorado, 1999

Sajer, Guy, *The Forgotten Soldier*, London, 1999

Salisbury, Harrison L., *The 900 Days: the Siege of Leningrad*, London, 2000

Schneidereit, Otto, *Zwischen zwei Weltkriegen. Eine Jugend in Ostpreussen*, Berlin, 1999

Shneidmann, N. K., *Jerusalem of Lithuania*, Oakville, Ontario, 1995

Smith, Howard, *Last Train from Berlin*, London, 1942

Surminski, Arno, *Klein schöner Land*, Munich, 1991

Taylor, Neil, *et al.*, *Baltic Capitals*, Chalfont St Peter, 2001

Terpitz, Werner, *Wege aus dem Osten*, Munich, 1997

Tilitzki, Christian, *Alltag in Ostpreussen 1940–45*, Würzburg, 2000

Tsouras, Peter G., *Fighting in Hell: The German Ordeal on the Eastern Front*, New York, 1995

Wanh, Martin, *Hitler and the Holocaust: The Hidden Story*, Philadelphia, 2001

Wiechert, Ernst, *The Simple Life*, Munich, 1954

Wieck, Michael, *A Childhood under Hitler and Stalin: Memoirs of a Certified Jew*, Wisconsin, 2003

Wieder, Joachim, and Heinrich Graf von Einsiedel, *Stalingrad, Memories and Re-assessments*, London, 1993

Wistrich, Robert Solomon, *Who's Who in Nazi Germany*, London, 2001

Wormell, Sebastian (ed.), *Poland*, Pallas, 2002

de Zayas, Alfred M., *Nemesis at Potsdam*, London, 1977

INDEX